DEADLY DISEASES AND EPIDEMICS

ANTIBIOTIC-
RESISTANT
BACTERIA

DEADLY DISEASES AND EPIDEMICS

Anthrax

Antibiotic-resistant Bacteria

Avian Flu

Botulism

Campylobacteriosis

Cervical Cancer

Cholera

Ebola

Encephalitis

Escherichia coli Infections

Gonorrhea

Hantavirus Pulmonary Syndrome

Helicobacter pylori

Hepatitis

Herpes

HIV/AIDS

Infectious Fungi

Influenza

Legionnaires' Disease

Leprosy

Lyme Disease

Lung Cancer

Mad Cow Disease (Bovine Spongiform Encephalopathy)

Malaria

Meningitis

Mononucleosis

Pelvic Inflammatory Disease

Plague

Polio

Prostate Cancer

Rabies

Salmonella

SARS

Smallpox

Staphylococcus aureus Infections

Streptococcus (Group A)

Syphilis

Toxic Shock Syndrome

Tuberculosis

Tularemia

Typhoid Fever

West Nile Virus

DEADLY DISEASES AND EPIDEMICS

ANTIBIOTIC-RESISTANT BACTERIA

Patrick G. Guilfoile, Ph.D.

FOUNDING EDITOR
The Late I. **Edward Alcamo**
Distinguished Teaching Professor of Microbiology,
SUNY Farmingdale

FOREWORD BY
David Heymann
World Health Organization

CHELSEA HOUSE
PUBLISHERS
An imprint of Infobase Publishing

Dedicated to Ed Alcamo

Antibiotic-Resistant Bacteria

Copyright © 2007 by Infobase Publishing

Chelsea House
An imprint of Infobase Publishing
132 West 31st Street
New York NY 10001

Library of Congress Cataloging-in-Publication Data

Guilfoile, Patrick.
    Antibiotic-resistant bacteria / Patrick G. Guilfoile ; consulting editor,
I. Edward Alcamo ; forward by David Heymann.
        p. cm.—(Deadly diseases and epidemics)
    Includes bibliographical references.
    ISBN 0-7910-9188-0 (hc : alk. paper)
    1. Drug resistance in microorganisms—Juvenile literature. I. Alcamo, I.
Edward. II. Title. III. Series.
QR177.G85 2006
616.9'041—dc22   2006017589

Series design by Terry Mallon
Cover design by Keith Trego

Printed in the United States of America

Bang EJB 10 9 8 7 6 5 4 3 2 1

Table of Contents

Foreword

In the 1960s, many of the infectious diseases that had terrorized generations were tamed. After a century of advances, the leading killers of Americans both young and old were being prevented with new vaccines or cured with new medicines. The risk of death from pneumonia, tuberculosis (TB), meningitis, influenza, whooping cough, and diphtheria declined dramatically. New vaccines lifted the fear that summer would bring polio, and a global campaign was on the verge of eradicating smallpox worldwide. New pesticides like DDT cleared mosquitoes from homes and fields, thus reducing the incidence of malaria, which was present in the southern United States and which remains a leading killer of children worldwide. New technologies produced safe drinking water and removed the risk of cholera and other water-borne diseases. Science seemed unstoppable. Disease seemed destined to all but disappear.

But the euphoria of the 1960s has evaporated.

The microbes fought back. Those causing diseases like TB and malaria evolved resistance to cheap and effective drugs. The mosquito developed the ability to defuse pesticides. New diseases emerged, including AIDS, Legionnaires', and Lyme disease. And diseases which had not been seen in decades re-emerged, as the hantavirus did in the Navajo Nation in 1993. Technology itself actually created new health risks. The global transportation network, for example, meant that diseases like West Nile virus could spread beyond isolated regions and quickly become global threats. Even modern public health protections sometimes failed, as they did in 1993 in Milwaukee, Wisconsin, resulting in 400,000 cases of the digestive system illness cryptosporidiosis. And, more recently, the threat from smallpox, a disease believed to be completely eradicated, has returned along with other potential bioterrorism weapons such as anthrax.

The lesson is that the fight against infectious diseases will never end.

In our constant struggle against disease, we as individuals have a weapon that does not require vaccines or drugs, and that is the ware-house of knowledge. We learn from the history of science that "modern" beliefs can be wrong. In this series of books, for example, you will learn that diseases like syphilis were once thought to be caused by eating potatoes. The invention of the microscope set science on the right path. There are more positive lessons from history. For example, smallpox was eliminated by vaccinating everyone who had come in contact with an infected person. This "ring" approach to smallpox control is still the preferred method for confronting an outbreak, should the disease be intentionally reintroduced.

At the same time, we are constantly adding new drugs, new vaccines, and new information to the warehouse. Recently, the entire human genome was decoded. So too was the genome of the parasite that causes malaria. Perhaps by looking at the microbe and the victim through the lens of genetics we will be able to discover new ways to fight malaria, which remains the leading killer of children in many countries.

Because of advances in our understanding of such diseases as AIDS, entire new classes of antiretroviral drugs have been developed. But resistance to all these drugs has already been detected, so we know that AIDS drug development must continue.

Education, experimentation, and the discoveries that grow out of them are the best tools to protect health. Opening this book may put you on the path of discovery. I hope so, because new vaccines, new antibiotics, new technologies, and, most importantly, new scientists are needed now more than ever if we are to remain on the winning side of this struggle against microbes.

David Heymann
Executive Director
Communicable Diseases Section
World Health Organization
Geneva, Switzerland

Preface

Life Before Antibiotics

If you research your family history prior to the 1940s, you are likely to find some relatives who died, or had a close brush with death, at a young age. In many cases, those deaths or near deaths resulted from what were, at the time, untreatable bacterial infections. My personal family history has an example of the toll bacterial infections took in the days prior to the development of antibiotics.

My grandfather, born in 1903, was a robust young man who grew strong working on the family farm. At the age of 12, he suddenly came down with a high fever and a sharp pain in his abdomen. A trip to the doctor in the back of a horse-drawn wagon was the closest thing to an ambulance in rural Wisconsin in those days. After a 10-mile ride over rough roads, he arrived at the doctor's office, where the doctor confirmed that my grandfather's appendix had ruptured. Following another rough ride to the hospital, my grandfather underwent emergency surgery to remove the offending organ, but he had already developed a serious bacterial infection in his abdomen. There was no treatment available aside from bed rest and hope. His fever by this time was very high, probably over 104°F. The doctor said his condition was grave; he had less than a 50 percent chance of pulling through. Obviously, you can guess the end of the story, since I wouldn't be writing this book if my grandfather hadn't recovered. However, one of my grandfather's brothers wasn't so lucky. His appendix had ruptured the previous year, and after a long stay in the hospital, he ultimately died from a bacterial infection.

Today, we often regard bacterial infections as a minor nuisance, at worst requiring a trip to the doctor and the pharmacy, but, up until the 1950s, many bacterial infections were lethal. In fact, people born in the United States in 1900 had about a 1 percent chance of dying from infectious disease in a given year. One hundred years later, that risk was down to 1 percent per 15 years, and a significant part of that reduced risk of death was due to the availability of antibiotics.[1]

Unfortunately, numerous species of bacteria have become increasingly resistant to antibiotics over the past several decades.

Many scientists, doctors, and healthcare professionals now wonder if we are returning to a situation where many bacterial infections will be untreatable. This book is designed to explore that question, and provide some ideas of what individuals can do to keep that grim scenario from becoming a reality.

1
What Are Antibiotics?

The first effective antibacterial agents, the sulfonamides, were developed in the 1930s and are still used today. These drugs only killed a limited number of bacterial species and had no effect on many important disease-causing microbes. The use of penicillin and other antibiotics, beginning in the 1940s, revolutionized the practice of medicine, because these drugs were able to stop many otherwise deadly **pathogens** (organisms that cause disease) in their tracks.

THE DISCOVERY OF PENICILLIN

Sir Alexander Fleming was a microbiologist at St. Mary's Hospital in London (Figure 1.1). During the late 1920s he was studying an important human pathogen, *Staphylococcus aureus*. During the summer of 1928, Fleming went on an extended vacation, and he left some cultures of *S. aureus* in petri plates on his lab bench. When Fleming returned from his vacation, he briefly checked the plates that had been sitting out. Initially, he discarded the now-famous plate into a tray of disinfectant. Fortunately, he had such a large pile of discarded plates that they didn't all get submerged in the antibacterial liquid. A colleague then appeared in the lab, and to make a point, Fleming picked up the famous plate and happened to notice something unusual. On that plate a mold (now called *Penicillium notatum*) had grown. Surrounding this fungus was a clear zone, where the *S. aureus* had been killed (Figure 1.2). Fleming had previously done work with other substances that killed bacteria, and he quickly recognized the significance of his observation.[2]

Following his discovery, Fleming made some crude extracts of the material from the fungus and found that this material killed many

Figure 1.1 Sir Alexander Fleming (National Library of Medicine/Photo Researchers, Inc.)

different types of important pathogenic bacteria. He also found he could inject this crude penicillin extract into rabbits, and the rabbits weren't harmed. However, Fleming wasn't able to extract and purify a significant amount of penicillin, so his discovery languished for the next 10 years.

In 1938, three other English Scientists—Howard Florey, Ernst Chain, and Norman Heatley—started working on producing large amounts of penicillin. Despite the outbreak of

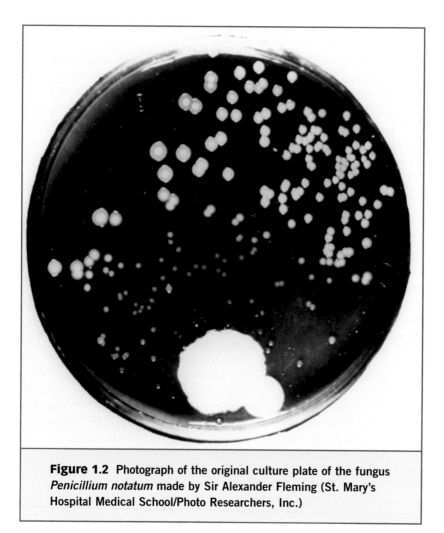

Figure 1.2 Photograph of the original culture plate of the fungus *Penicillium notatum* made by Sir Alexander Fleming (St. Mary's Hospital Medical School/Photo Researchers, Inc.)

World War II they had made substantial progress by 1941. By then, however, German planes were regularly attacking England, and there was concern that work on penicillin in Britain would be difficult under wartime conditions. Consequently, Florey and Heatley traveled to the United States to gain support for the large-scale production of penicillin and to assist with the process. A series of incremental improvements involving new fungal strains, better growth media, and other developments finally led to the production of enough peni-cillin to treat soldiers wounded in the D-Day invasion in 1944.

As early as 1941, Florey and Chain had isolated sufficient penicillin to test the antibiotic in a few patients. The first per-son treated with purified penicillin was Albert Alexander, a London policeman, who had cut his face and developed a severe bacterial infection. The rampant infection caused **abscesses** covering his head, which were so severe that they necessitated the removal of one eye. He was treated with sul-fonamides, but with no effect. His fever was 105°F and he was close to death. Because of his grave state, permission was granted to Florey and Chain to give Mr. Alexander penicillin. After the first few doses, he quickly improved: his fever went down dramatically and he appeared to be recovering. However, penicillin was in very short supply, and after five days of treat-ment, the supply was exhausted. In the absence of the antibi-otic, *S. aureus* started churning out toxins again, and Mr. Alexander died five days after the treatment ended. [3]

The first use of penicillin in the United States was, how-ever, fully successful. A young woman, Anne Miller, had a mis-carriage and subsequently developed a streptococcal infection. She had been hospitalized for more than a month and her condition steadily deteriorated. Her fever spiked to over 106°F, and she was near death. Fortunately, one of her physicians knew a friend of Howard Florey, and through that friend man-aged to get a small amount of penicillin. Miller was given penicillin every four hours, but so little was available that the supply rapidly dwindled. Her urine was collected and sent to the Merck pharmaceutical company for processing, since about 70 percent of the original dose of penicillin could be recovered from the urine. This re-processed penicillin was used, and Ms. Miller survived, living for another 57 years before she passed away in 1999. Without penicillin, it is almost certain she would have have died in 1942. [4]

Figure 1.3 Colored scanning electron micrograph (SEM) of penicillum with spores (Biophoto Associates/Photo Researchers, Inc.)

Subsequently, penicillin became widely used for treating a range of bacterial diseases. Yet only 10 years later, in 1952, up to three-fifths of *S. aureus* infections in some hospitals were resistant to penicillin. This miracle drug was already becoming ineffective for treating some bacterial infections, less than 10 years after it became widely used.

Antibiotics are truly wonder drugs, and today they cure thousands of infected people each day. But what are they? Antibiotics are small molecules usually produced by bacteria or fungi that kill bacteria without harming the person or animal being treated. Chemically synthesized compounds are sometimes called antibacterial agents, but in this book, both synthetic and naturally produced antibacterial compounds will be called antibiotics. Antibiotics are distinguished from

antiseptics (antibacterial chemical agents, such as detergents, only suitable for application to the skin) and **disinfectants** (strong antibacterial chemicals, such as bleach, only suitable for treating inanimate objects). Antibiotics are also distinguished from antifungal agents, which specifically kill molds and yeasts, and antiviral agents, which prevent viruses from replicating. Antibiotics are only effective on bacteria; they do not kill viruses such as HIV or fungi, like those that cause athlete's foot.

Actinomycetes, a type of **filamentous bacteria**, produce many antibiotics including cephamycins, erythromycin, gentamicin, kanamycin, rifampin, streptogramins, streptomycin, tetracycline, and vancomycin. Other types of bacteria produce bacitracin, gramicidin, mupirocin, monobactams, and polymixin B. Fungi produce the antibiotics penicillin and cephalosporin. To date, most antibiotics have been isolated from microbes that live in soil. Some antibiotics are produced either partially or completely using chemical manipulations in a laboratory; examples include fosfomycin, linezolid, fluoroquinolones (including ciprofloxacin), sulfamethoxazole, trimethoprim, metronidazole, and furazolidinone.

TYPES OF ANTIBIOTICS

Antibiotics can be classified in a variety of ways. One classification scheme, discussed in the next chapter, is based on how antibiotics attack bacteria. Another method, described below, is based on their chemical shape.

One group of antibiotics, called **β-lactams**, contains a highly active "chemical warhead," as described by Christopher Walsh (Figure 1.4).[5] These antibiotics mimic a section of the bacterial cell wall, and they inactivate enzymes normally involved in assembling that cellular structure. Without a cell wall, most bacteria will burst open and die. There are four subgroups in this chemical category: penicillins, cephalosporins, carbapenems, and monbactams. Penicillins include the original drug, along with modified versions including ampicillin,

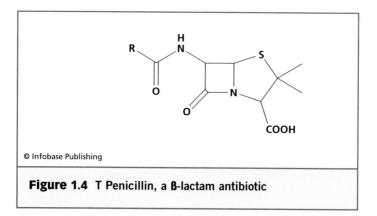

Figure 1.4 T Penicillin, a ß-lactam antibiotic

amoxicillin, and methicillin. Cephalosporins include cephalothin, cefoxitin, ceftazidime, and cefipime. Carbapenems include thienamycin and imipenem. Monobactams include aztreonam.

Another group of antibiotics are **tetracylines**, so named because they contain a four-ring structure (Figure 1.5). Tetracycline, oxytetracycline, doxycycline, and minocycline are members of this class. A chemically related antibiotic, Tygacil (tigecycline) was approved for use in the United States in June

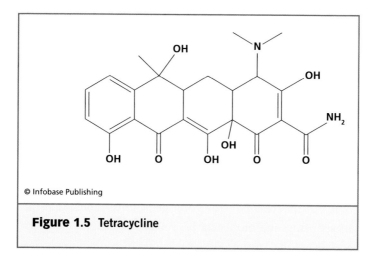

Figure 1.5 Tetracycline

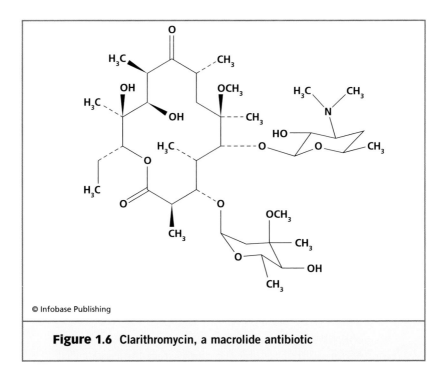

© Infobase Publishing

Figure 1.6 Clarithromycin, a macrolide antibiotic

of 2005. Tetracyclines prevent bacterial cells from making proteins. Bacteria unable to make proteins will no longer grow or
divide, providing time for the immune system to destroy them.

A third major group of antibiotics are the **aminoglycosides**. Aminoglycosides have sugars (glycosides) with amino
groups (NH_2) attached, thus earning the name. Aminoglycosides include streptomycin, gentamicin, and kanamycin.
Aminoglycosides prevent bacterial cells from making properly
functioning proteins. The presence of these malformed proteins is frequently lethal to the bacterial cell.

Macrolides represent another important group of antibiotics. As the name suggests, these compounds contain a large
(macro) ring structure (Figure 1.6). Members of this group
include erythromycin, clarithromycin, and azithromycin.
Macrolides, like tetracyclines, prevent bacteria from making
proteins.

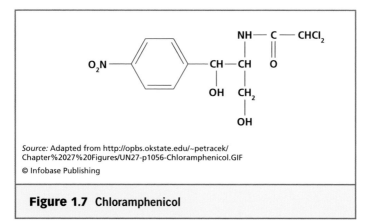

Source: Adapted from http://opbs.okstate.edu/~petracek/
Chapter%2027%20Figures/UN27-p1056-Chloramphenicol.GIF
© Infobase Publishing

Figure 1.7 Chloramphenicol

Quinolones represent a fifth class of antibiotics. Members of this group include naladixic acid, ciprofloxacin, levofloxacin, and gatifloxacin. These antibiotics cause bacteria to cut their own DNA, but prevent them from repairing the damage. Consequently, the bacteria die because intact DNA is required for normal cellular function. Other antibiotics that don't fit neatly into another group include rifampin, which prevents bacteria from making RNA. The lack of RNA production shuts down essential cellular processes, and is lethal for the cell. **Chloramphenicol** (Figure 1.7) and **streptogrammins**, which inhibit protein synthesis, **bacitracin**, which inhibits cell wall synthesis, and **polymyxin** (Figure 1.8), which damages bacterial membranes, are other miscellaneous antibiotics. In the case of polymixin, intact membranes are essential for regulating the movement of materials in and out of the cell. Cells treated with polymixin lose the ability to control that movement, and consequently, they die.

In addition to rifampin, a variety of other antibiotics of different chemical classes are used almost exclusively to treat infections caused by *Mycobacterium tuberculosis*. These drugs include ethambutol, isoniazid, and pyrazinamide.

Many antibiotics are currently produced by large-scale fermentation of fungal or bacterial cultures. The antibiotic-

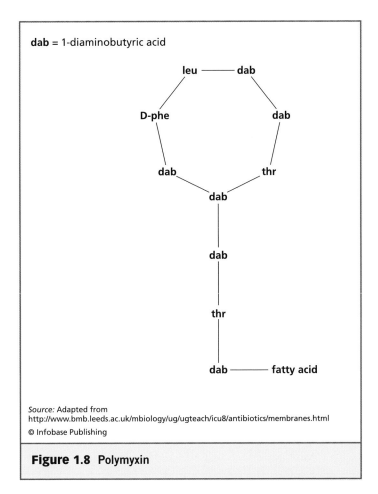

dab = 1-diaminobutyric acid

Source: Adapted from
http://www.bmb.leeds.ac.uk/mbiology/ug/ugteach/icu8/antibiotics/membranes.html
© Infobase Publishing

Figure 1.8 Polymyxin

producing organism is grown in vats containing thousands of liters of **growth medium** (a mixture of nutrients designed to allow cell growth), and incubated under conditions designed to maximize the production of the antibiotic. After the growth process is complete, the antibiotic is separated from the rest of the culture. This typically involves both physical methods (like filtering) and chemical methods (like extraction with organic solvents) to yield a highly purified antibiotic. In many cases, the antibiotic producer is mutated or genetically altered to more efficiently produce the antibiotic.

The rapid development of antibiotic resistance has led to a continual need to develop new antibiotics (see Table 1.1). In recent years, the pace of new antibiotic development has

Table 1.1 Date when an antibiotic became available and when resistance was first reported[5]

	INTRODUCED	RESISTANCE OCCURRED
Sulfonamides	1930s	1940s
Penicillin	1943	1946
Streptomycin	1943	1948
Bacitracin	1945	1953
Chloramphenicol	1947	1959
Cephalosporin	1960s	late 1960s
Neomycin	1949	1950
Tetracycline	1948	1953
Erythromycin	1952	1988
Vancomycin	1956	1988
Kanamycin	1957	1966
Methicillin	1960	1961
Ampicillin	1961	1973
Gentamicin	1963	1969
Carbenicillin	1964	1974
Clindamycin	1969	1970
Amoxicillin	1972	1975
Piperacillin	1980	1981
Augmentin	1984	1984
Aztreonam	1984	1985
Imipenem	1985	1985
Ciprofloxacin	1987	1987
Quinupristin-Dalfopristin	1999	2000
Linezolid	2000	2002

slowed, and this has raised concerns that some microbes may regain the upper hand when they cause infections.

ANTIBIOTIC-REQUIRING BACTERIA?

Antibiotics are typically very efficient at killing bacteria, yet scientists have isolated mutant bacteria that can't grow in the absence of a particular antibiotic. As one example, several strains of *Escherichia coli*, a common intestinal bacterium, were found to require the antibiotic streptomycin in order to grow. As described in the next chapter, streptomycin prevents the protein-making machinery of a cell, the ribosome, from properly making proteins. Normally, ribosomes operate fast enough to produce sufficient proteins, but slow enough to produce most proteins accurately. Streptomycin interferes with this process by reducing the accuracy of protein synthesis. The *E. coli* strains that require streptomycin have mutations that make their ribosomes hyper-accurate, but too slow to sustain life. However, in the presence of streptomycin, the ribosomes strike a more normal balance between accuracy and speed, and the cell can survive.

2

How Do Antibiotics Kill Bacteria?

Imagine that you are a bacterial cell. Water molecules now are relatively large; a few bouncing into your side can jiggle you around quite a bit. For such a small creature, you have well-developed senses; for example, you can readily detect the bacterial equivalent of food and move toward that nutrient source. One of your key features is a tough "skin," a cell wall made of a material unique to bacteria, called **peptidoglycan**. Now imagine that you suddenly find yourself in a solution of the antibiotic penicillin. In short order, your cell wall develops large gaps and loses its structural integrity. Water floods in, your cellular material can no longer be contained, and you explode. Such is the life (and death) of a bacterium susceptible to penicillin.

HUMAN CELLS VERSUS BACTERIAL CELLS

To understand how antibiotics work, it is critical that you understand something about bacterial (**prokaryotic**) cells and how they differ from human (**eukaryotic**) cells. In most modern schemes for classifying organisms, there is a consensus that there are two fundamentally different kinds of living things—bacteria and everything else (Figure 2.1). Consequently, there are many differences between your cells and the cells of a bacterium. That is a very good thing, because it means that there are many targets on bacterial cells on which antibiotics can act without harming human cells. This is a key to understanding how antibiotics work: They target a structure or process found uniquely in bacterial cells.

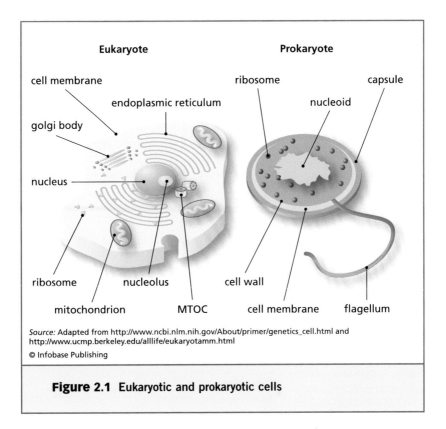

Figure 2.1 Eukaryotic and prokaryotic cells

The most common targets for antibiotics are the bacterial cell wall, the bacterial **ribosome**, **DNA replication**, **RNA synthesis**, and specific enzyme pathways.

TEARING DOWN THE WALLS

Under most conditions, bacteria die without an intact cell wall. Since human cells completely lack a cell wall, this is an important target for antibiotics. To understand how these antibiotics work, though, it's necessary to understand how bacteria make cell walls. There are several steps in the process. Initially the "building blocks" (N-acetyl glucosamine and N-acetyl muramic acid) of the cell wall are made in the cytoplasm (the

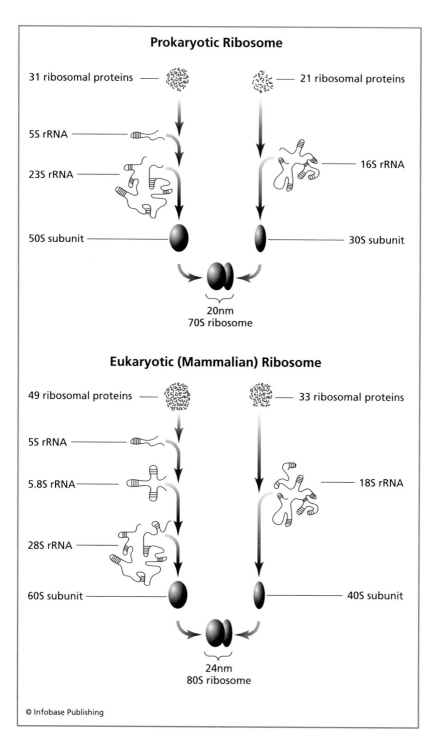

fluid that fills cells). These building blocks are then transported across the cell membrane using a carrier molecule, where they are next joined to an existing long chain of building blocks (in a process called **transglycosylation**) and are crosslinked to another long chain (in a process called **transpeptidation**). Bacteria make new cell wall material only when they are growing. Therefore, antibiotics that disrupt this process are typically only effective on growing cells.

Different antibiotics target different steps in cell-wall synthesis; for example, penicillin inhibits transpeptidation. Vancomycin inhibits transglycosylation and transpeptidation. Bacitracin inhibits the regeneration of the carrier required for moving the building blocks of the cell wall across the membrane.

TURNING OFF THE PROTEIN FACTORY

Living and growing cells require a constant supply of new proteins. Without new proteins, a cell will either stop growing, or it may even die. In both bacterial and human cells, new proteins are manufactured on ribosomes, in a process called translation. However, bacterial ribosomes differ enough from human ribosomes that antibiotics can effectively target them (Figure 2.2).

Ribosomes require messenger RNA (mRNA), transfer RNA (tRNA), and amino acids (the building blocks of proteins) in order to make proteins. During translation, the ribosome slides along the mRNA in three-nucleotide steps; tRNAs bring in the appropriate amino acids to allow the protein to be made.

Streptomycin is an example of an antibiotic that targets the ribosome. This antibiotic binds to a ribosomal protein and

Figure 2.2 (left) Macromolecular composition of prokaryotic and eukaryotic ribosomes

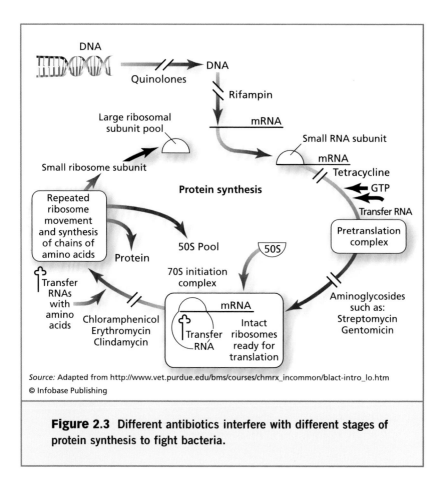

Source: Adapted from http://www.vet.purdue.edu/bms/courses/chmrx_incommon/blact-intro_lo.htm
© Infobase Publishing

Figure 2.3 Different antibiotics interfere with different stages of protein synthesis to fight bacteria.

interferes with the movement of the ribosome along the mRNA. As a consequence, streptomycin makes protein synthesis less accurate. Erythromycin is another example of an antibiotic that binds to ribosomal RNA. Erythromycin terminates protein synthesis prematurely, meaning that few, if any, functional proteins are produced by the cell. Tetracycline binds to the ribosome and interferes with a new tRNA (containing an amino acid) coming into the ribosome (Figure 2.3).

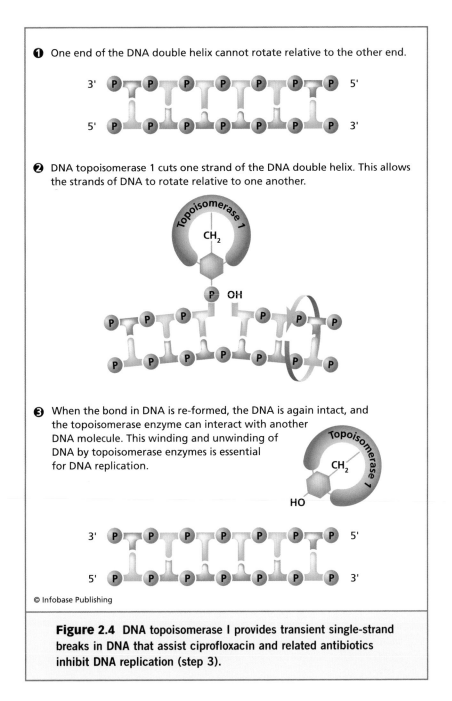

❶ One end of the DNA double helix cannot rotate relative to the other end.

❷ DNA topoisomerase 1 cuts one strand of the DNA double helix. This allows the strands of DNA to rotate relative to one another.

❸ When the bond in DNA is re-formed, the DNA is again intact, and the topoisomerase enzyme can interact with another DNA molecule. This winding and unwinding of DNA by topoisomerase enzymes is essential for DNA replication.

© Infobase Publishing

Figure 2.4 DNA topoisomerase I provides transient single-strand breaks in DNA that assist ciprofloxacin and related antibiotics inhibit DNA replication (step 3).

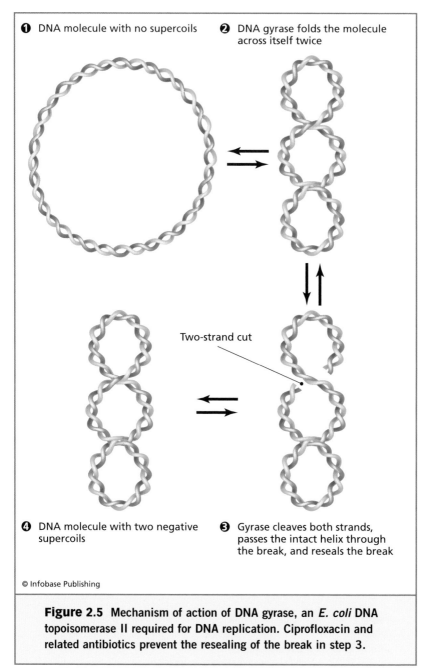

❶ DNA molecule with no supercoils

❷ DNA gyrase folds the molecule across itself twice

Two-strand cut

❹ DNA molecule with two negative supercoils

❸ Gyrase cleaves both strands, passes the intact helix through the break, and reseals the break

Figure 2.5 Mechanism of action of DNA gyrase, an *E. coli* DNA topoisomerase II required for DNA replication. Ciprofloxacin and related antibiotics prevent the resealing of the break in step 3.

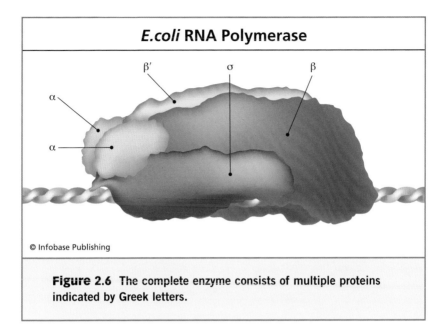

Figure 2.6 The complete enzyme consists of multiple proteins indicated by Greek letters.

TARGETING THE BACTERIAL INFORMATION CENTERS—ANTIBIOTICS THAT INHIBIT DNA OR RNA SYNTHESIS

DNA Synthesis

In order for a cell to divide, it must copy its DNA. An antibiotic that prevents DNA synthesis will therefore keep a bacterial population from growing, and may kill affected cells. Copying DNA in a cell is a complex process. The DNA synthesis machinery includes enzymes called **DNA gyrase** and **topoisomerase**, which help twist and untwist DNA during replication. These enzymes accomplish this feat by cutting the DNA, then "gluing" the cut ends back together (Figure 2.4, 2.5). A similar process occurs in human cells, but the bacterial and human enzymes involved are different enough that some antibiotics can target the bacterial enzymes without affecting the human enzymes.

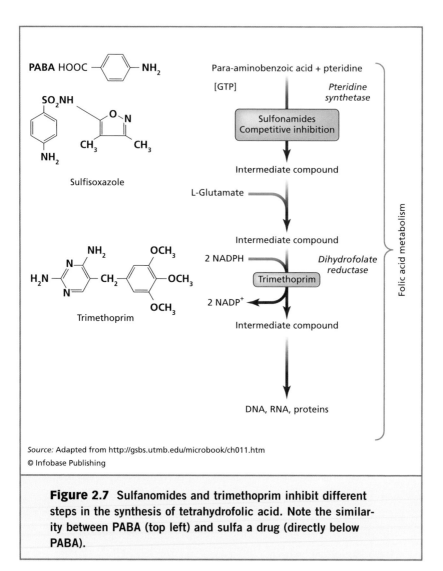

Source: Adapted from http://gsbs.utmb.edu/microbook/ch011.htm
© Infobase Publishing

Figure 2.7 Sulfanomides and trimethoprim inhibit different steps in the synthesis of tetrahydrofolic acid. Note the similarity between PABA (top left) and sulfa a drug (directly below PABA).

Ciprofloxacin and related antibiotics work by allowing topoisomerases to cut DNA but not "glue" the ends back together (Figure 2.4, 2.5). The result is that the bacterium can no longer replicate its DNA, keeping the bacterial population in check. In addition, in some bacteria, this DNA damage may also activate a process that leads to the death of the bacterial cell.

RNA Synthesis

Bacteria must continuously make RNA in order to survive. RNA plays many roles in the cell, including acting as a messenger between the information coded in the DNA and the protein-making ribosomes. RNA synthesis requires an enzyme called RNA polymerase, and this enzyme is critical in all types of cells. RNA polymerases differ enough between bacteria and human cells that the bacterial version can be targeted by some antibiotics (figure 2.6). The antibiotic rifampin, for example, binds to bacterial RNA polymerase and prevents it from making RNA. Consequently, this leads to a loss of new protein synthesis. Since a continuous supply of new proteins is typically required for cellular survival, these antibiotics cause the death of the bacterial cell.

KEEPING BACTERIA HUNGRY—INHIBITING BIOCHEMICAL PATHWAYS

Folic acid is an essential vitamin that is required for many chemical reactions inside cells. Humans get folic acid from our diet; bacteria make their own from scratch. This difference helps explain why another group of antibiotics, the sulfonamides, are able to selectively kill bacteria. Sulfonamides work by mimicking the compound used by bacteria to make folic acid (para-amino benzoic acid or PABA). The sulfa drugs bind to an enzyme that is required to convert PABA to tetrahydrofolic acid and disable the enzyme so it can no longer function (Figure 2.7).

Sulfonamides are often given together with another antibiotic, trimethoprim, which inhibits a different stage of folic acid synthesis. In this case, the enzymes are found in both bacteria and humans, but the enzymes are different enough that trimethoprim binds to the bacterial enzyme with 60,000 times higher **affinity** (preference) for the bacterial versus human enzyme.[6] The use of these two antibiotics provides double the assurance that the pathway will be

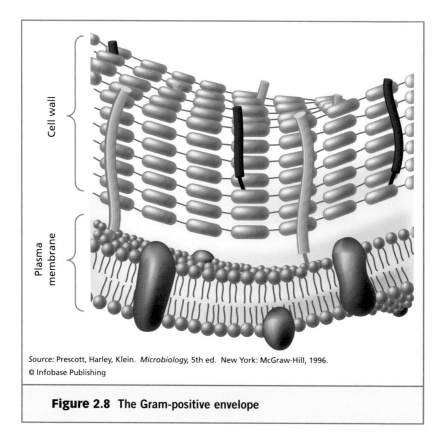

Source: Prescott, Harley, Klein. *Microbiology,* 5th ed. New York: McGraw-Hill, 1996.
© Infobase Publishing

Figure 2.8 The Gram-positive envelope

disabled and reduces the likelihood of resistance developing
(Figure 2.7).

CELL WALL COMPONENT SYNTHESIS INHIBITORS

A more restricted class of antibiotics, which work only on
Mycobacterium tuberculosis and closely related bacteria,
interfere with synthesis of components of the mycobacterial
cell wall. One of these drugs, isoniazid, is an inactive chemical until it enters the bacterial cell. *M. tuberculosis* contains
an enzyme that activates the antibiotic, which then goes on
to damage enzymes that would otherwise assist in synthesiz-
ing the mycobacterial cell wall. Another drug, ethambutanol,

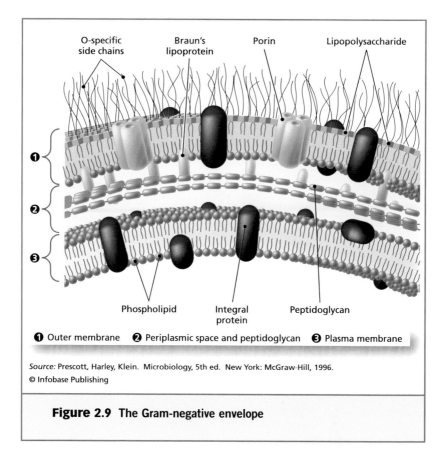

O-specific side chains

Braun's lipoprotein

Porin

Lipopolysaccharide

❶

❷

❸

Phospholipid

Integral protein

Peptidoglycan

❶ Outer membrane   ❷ Periplasmic space and peptidoglycan   ❸ Plasma membrane

Source: Prescott, Harley, Klein. Microbiology, 5th ed. New York: McGraw-Hill, 1996.
© Infobase Publishing

Figure 2.9 The Gram-negative envelope

inhibits the synthesis of a different component of the mycobacterial cell wall.

MEMBRANE DISRUPTION

The presence of an intact membrane is critical for cellular survival. The cell membrane acts as a barrier between the organism and the environment, preventing the loss of essential chemicals. Therefore, antibiotics that destroy membrane integrity should be very effective. Unfortunately, the membranes surrounding bacterial and human cells are quite similar, which is why antibiotics that target bacterial membranes

Table 2.1 Antibiotic Spectrum of Activity[7]

Antibiotics that primarily work on Gram-positive bacteria:	
Bacitracin	Penicillin
Clindamycin	Vancomycin
Methicillin	
Antibiotics that primarily work on Gram-negative bacteria:	
Gentamicin	Polymixin B
Antibiotics that work on Gram-positive and Gram-negative bacteria:	
Ampicillin	Erythromycin
Carbenicillin	Streptomycin
Cephalosporins	Sulfonamides
Chloramphenicol	Tetracyclines
Ciprofloxacin	Trimethoprim
Antibiotics that work primarily on the acid-fast organism, *Mycobacterium tuberculosis*:	
Cycloserine	Isoniazid
Ethambutol	*p*-Aminosalicylic acid
Ethionamide	Pyrazinamide

also tend to harm human cells. Consequently, such antibiotics are typically restricted to use on the skin, the outer layer of which consists of dead cells that are unaffected by these antibiotics. Polymixin is an example of an antibiotic that disrupts cell membranes.

ANTIBIOTIC SPECTRUM OF ACTIVITY

Two major categories of pathogenic bacteria are Gram positives and Gram negatives (Figure 2.9, 2.10). During Gram staining, Gram-positive bacteria retain a dye called crystal

Table 2.2 Summary of the mechanisms of action for different antibiotic classes

Antibiotic Class (Example)	Mechanism of Action
Aminoglycosides (Streptomycin)	Inhibit protein synthesis
Cephalosporins (Ceftazidime)	Inhibit cell wall synthesis
Chloramphenicol	Inhibit protein synthesis
Glycopeptides (Vancomycin)	Inhibit cell wall synthesis
Lincosamides (Clindamycin)	Inhibit protein synthesis
Macrolides (Erythromycin)	Inhibit protein synthesis
Penicillins (Ampicillin)	Inhibit cell wall synthesis
Oxazolidinones (Linezolid)	Inhibit protein synthesis
Quinolones (Ciprofloxacin)	Inhibit DNA synthesis
Rifamycins (Rifampin)	Inhibit RNA synthesis
Streptogramins (Synercid)	Inhibit protein synthesis
Sulfonamides (Sulfamethoxazole)	Inhibit a biochemical pathway (Folic Acid synthesis)
Tetracyclines (Doxycycline)	Inhibit protein synthesis

violet, giving them a purple color when viewed through the microscope. In contrast, during Gram staining, Gram-negative bacteria don't stain with the purple dye, but they do stain with another dye called safranin, giving them a pink color when viewed through a microscope. These two types of bacteria fundamentally differ in terms of their cell envelope. In particular, Gram negatives have both an outer and inner membrane and a thin cell wall, whereas Gram positives have only an inner membrane and a thick cell wall. As a consequence, they differ in terms of antibiotic uptake, and therefore some antibiotics are more effective in one of these groups than the other. Gram-positive bacteria that are human pathogens include *S. aureus, Streptococcus pyogenes, Enterococcus faecalis,* and *Clostridium botulinum.* Gram-negative bacteria that are human pathogens include *E. coli, Salmonella enterica, Vibrio cholerae,* and *Pseudomonas aeruginosa.* A third type of bacteria, which are described as being acid-fast,

USE OF CIPROFLOXACIN TO TREAT PEOPLE POTENTIALLY EXPOSED TO ANTHRAX

In October of 2001, letters containing spores of the anthrax bacterium (*Bacillus anthracis*) were mailed to news organizations and legislators in the United States, resulting in the deaths of five people. Postal workers, legislators and their staff, and others who were potentially exposed to the spores were treated with either doxycycline or ciprofloxacin. Ciprofloxacin was a newer, more expensive drug, currently used to treat infections caused by bacteria resistant to other antibiotics. Doxycycline is older and inexpensive, but is less widely used since resistance to this drug is widespread. Both drugs are considered to be effective against anthrax, although only ciprofloxacin was specifically licensed for that purpose. Because ciprofloxacin is frequently used for otherwise resistant bacterial infections, there is a potential danger that people treated with this drug following the anthrax attacks may harbor resistant bacteria that, some day, may cause infections that will be difficult to treat.[8]

includes the important human pathogen, *M. tuberculosis.*
This organism has a waxy cell membrane/cell wall, which
retains a stain, even in the presence of acid and alcohol.
Because of this waxy outer coating, mycobacteria are resistant
to most antibiotics that kill Gram-positive or Gram-negative
bacteria.

3

How Do Bacteria Resist Antibiotics?

I don't remember the details, but I've been told that back in 1960, as an infant, I had minor surgery in a local hospital. Following the surgery, I developed a severe *Staphylococcus aureus* infection, which started at the abdominal incision and spread to my backside. Penicillin was widely available, and it should have been a routine matter for a few doses to clear up the infection. However, following the administration of penicillin and other antibiotics, instead of improving, my condition worsened. I had been infected with a strain of *S. aureus* that was resistant to penicillin and the other antibiotics available at the time. My fever was over 104°F. I couldn't eat or drink, and my only nourishment was through an intravenous (IV) tube. I slept little and my condition deteriorated. Fortunately, a new antibiotic, methicillin, had recently been developed. A few shots of this new antibiotic knocked down the infection. It took a long time for the sores to heal, but I was on the path to recovery. I still hear stories, though, about how my mother had to boil my diapers, sheets, and clothes for several months, during the hot humid summer, to make sure the infection didn't spread to others in the household.

Antibiotic resistance was reported very early in the development of these wonder drugs. Sir Alexander Fleming's original report in 1929 noted that some bacteria, including the microbe now called *Escherichia coli,* were resistant to the effect of penicillin. In 1940 Edward Abraham and Ernst Chain reported the presence of an enzyme in *E. coli* that destroyed penicillin. This was several years before the drug became widely used to treat patients. In fact, one of the difficulties in initially producing large

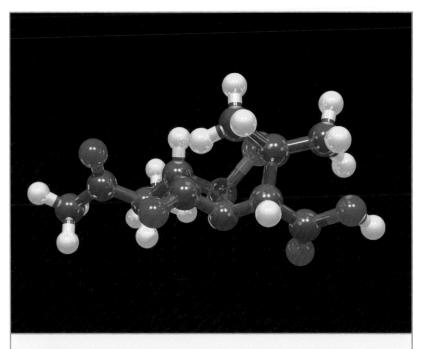

Figure 3.1 A computer graphic of a molecule of penicillin
(Alfred Pasieka/Photo Researchers, Inc.)

quantities of penicillin was that many of the original fungal
cultures were contaminated with bacteria that degraded the
antibiotic as it was produced. In the subsequent decades, bacterial antibiotic resistance has become a widespread and well-
studied phenomenon. From that work, it has become clear that
the mechanisms of antibiotic resistance normally fall into one
of several categories detailed below.

RESISTANCE DUE TO ANTIBIOTIC MODIFICATION
One of the first reports of antibiotic resistance involved bacteria that produced an enzyme that chemically inactivated penicillin. Since that time, a large number of bacterial strains have
been reported to produce enzymes that inactivate one or more
antibiotics. Penicillins, one member of the ß-lactam antibiotic

group, contain a chemically activated ring that is critically important for antibiotic function. Enzymes called ß-lactamases pull apart this ring, disabling the antibiotic. In some countries, up to 80 percent of certain species of bacteria are resistant to ampicillin, due to the acquisition of genes that produce ß-lactamases.

Several strategies have been developed to overcome this resistance mechanism. Some newer penicillins have been developed that are resistant to destruction from many types of ß-lactamases. Another strategy is to combine a penicillin with an inhibitor of ß-lactamases. This is available commercially as, in one example, Augmentin®, a combination of ampicillin and clavulanic acid, a ß-lactamase inhibitor. Unfortunately, bacteria haven't been sitting idly by as these developments have occurred. Some bacteria contain mutant versions of ß-lactamase enzymes that are capable of degrading many of the newer penicillins and related antibiotics.

DESTRUCTION OF STREPTOMYCIN AND RELATED DRUGS

Streptomycin belongs to another class of antibiotics, aminoglycosides, which have been widely used to treat infections. These antibiotics contain sugars with chemical "arms" that latch onto the bacterial ribosome, shutting off protein synthesis and killing the cell. One resistance mechanism to streptomycin and related drugs is for resistant bacteria to add chemical groups to the arms of these antibiotics. The addition of these chemical groups prevents the antibiotic from docking to the ribosome, and thus the antibiotic becomes ineffective (Figure 3.2).

TARGET SITE MODIFICATION

Another important antibiotic resistance mechanism is target site modification. This occurs in one of two ways. In one form, a mutation occurs in the gene that encodes an antibiotic target. In the other form, an enzyme chemically modifies the

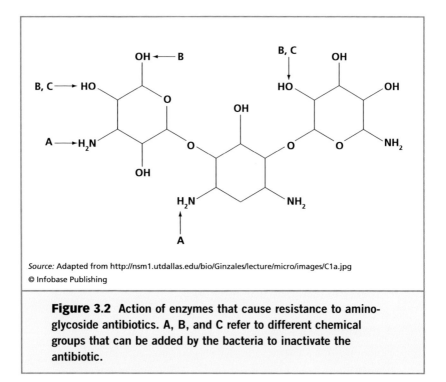

Source: Adapted from http://nsm1.utdallas.edu/bio/Ginzales/lecture/micro/images/C1a.jpg
© Infobase Publishing

Figure 3.2 Action of enzymes that cause resistance to amino-glycoside antibiotics. A, B, and C refer to different chemical groups that can be added by the bacteria to inactivate the antibiotic.

target of the antibiotic. Many examples of both forms of resistance have been discovered.

Penicillin and related antibiotics bind to proteins that help assemble the bacterial cell wall. Mutations in these proteins can prevent penicillin and related drugs from binding to them, but these proteins still function in stitching together the bacterial cell wall.

For many antibiotics that bind to the ribosome, **methylation** (the addition of a chemical group, CH_3) of specific ribosomal RNA allows the ribosome to continue to function in making proteins, but prevents antibiotics from binding to, and inhibiting the action of the ribosome. Ribosomal methylation is a resistance mechanism against streptomycin, erythromycin, streptogramins, and other antibiotics. In other cases, mutation of a ribosomal protein is sufficient to change the shape of the ribosome enough to prevent an antibiotic from functioning, while allowing the ribosome to churn out proteins. This mechanism protects some cells against the effects of streptomycin.

Mutations in the enzyme DNA gyrase, the target for ciprofloxacin and related antibiotics, can render bacterial cells resistant to those antibiotics. Similarly, mutations in RNA polymerase can cause resistance to rifampin and related drugs. These mutations occur at a high enough rate (one in a million to one in 10 million bacterial cells) that resistance to these drugs often develops readily. Keep in mind that, with some bacterial infections, a person may harbor more than one billion bacteria. Among those bacteria, between 100 and 1,000 would be expected to have a mutation that would result in resistance to that particular antibiotic.

A COMPLETE REMODEL OF THE CELL WALL

Vancomycin is an antibiotic that targets the bacterial cell wall, preventing it from forming properly. This antibiotic works by binding to a section of the building blocks of the cell wall called D-ala-D-ala (these are two unusual alanine amino acids). This D-ala-D-ala structure is normally essential to a bacterial cell wall: consider it analogous to 2" x 6" wall supports in the frame of a house. Imagine, as a homeowner, if you suddenly had to replace the 2" x 6" wood walls with steel beams. It would be a challenge to do that and keep the house intact during the process, yet this is essentially what happens when a bacterial cell becomes resistant to vancomycin. The D-ala-D-ala support (the 2" x 6" wooden studs) is replaced with a D-ala-D-lac support (the steel beams) (Figure 3.3, 3.4).

That kind of drastic change requires a major realignment in the cell. To pull it off, resistant cells must acquire five new genes (these genes come from other bacteria that are already resistant to the drug). These genes produce proteins that sense the presence of vancomycin and then build and assemble the

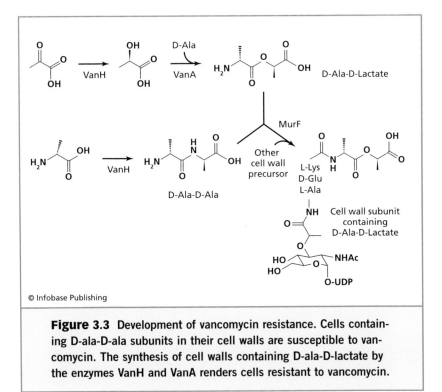

Figure 3.3 Development of vancomycin resistance. Cells containing D-ala-D-ala subunits in their cell walls are susceptible to vancomycin. The synthesis of cell walls containing D-ala-D-lactate by the enzymes VanH and VanA renders cells resistant to vancomycin.

new cell wall structures. The fact that bacteria have developed resistance to vancomycin shows how adaptable bacterial cells are when it comes to their survival.

In most of these cases involving target site modification leading to antibiotic resistance, the bacteria are walking a genetic tightrope. The structures or enzymes being mutated are typically essential for survival. Any mutation in these enzymes that leads to antibiotic resistance is also likely to cause some problems. Enzymes, for example, are normally exquisitely tuned to catalyze a chemical reaction, and any change is likely to make that catalysis less efficient. However, there is a huge advantage to antibiotic resistance in the presence of an antibiotic, so lower efficiency is a small price to pay for survival. However, these adaptable microbes often, over time, develop multiple mutations, which reduce the negative effect of the initial mutation while still allowing the bacteria to fend off the antibiotic. Consequently, resistant bacteria often become well adapted and have little or no survival disadvantage compared to bacteria that are sensitive to the antibiotic. This suggests that, in some cases, antibiotic resistance may continue to be a problem, even if the use of antibiotic is reduced.

TURNING BACK THE TIDE—ANTIBIOTIC PUMPS

Another widespread resistance mechanism relies on membrane-embedded protein pumps. These pumps require energy in some form and move the antibiotic out of the cell faster than it comes in. In many cases, these pumps allow some undesirable leakage of materials out of the cell. Expression of this type of antibiotic resistance is often regulated by the cell, so that it only occurs when the antibiotic is present. (The regulation of antibiotic resistance is described in more detail at the end of this chapter.) Some of these protein pumps apparently evolved from similar proteins that play a role in transporting metabolic by-products or other chemicals out of the cell.

One of the most common resistance mechanisms against tetracycline antibiotic are protein pumps. The pump protein is only made when the cell senses tetracycline. It binds to tetracycline and sends the antibiotic out of the cell, powered by hydrogen ions flowing back into the cell. These pumps do not appear to efficiently remove a related antibiotic, Tigecycline, from bacterial cells. This new antibiotic may therefore offer a mechanism for overcoming at least some forms of bacterial resistance.

In some cases, bacterial protein pumps are multipurpose, with a single membrane protein capable of pumping out several different drugs. For example, a membrane protein in the bacterial pathogen *Pseudomonas aeruginosa* is thought to pump out tetracyclines, ciprofloxacin, chloramphenicol, erythromycin, and penicillins and related drugs. *P. aeruginosa* has a number of other multidrug protein pumps, making it somewhat innately resistant to nearly every class of antibiotic. These multidrug resistance

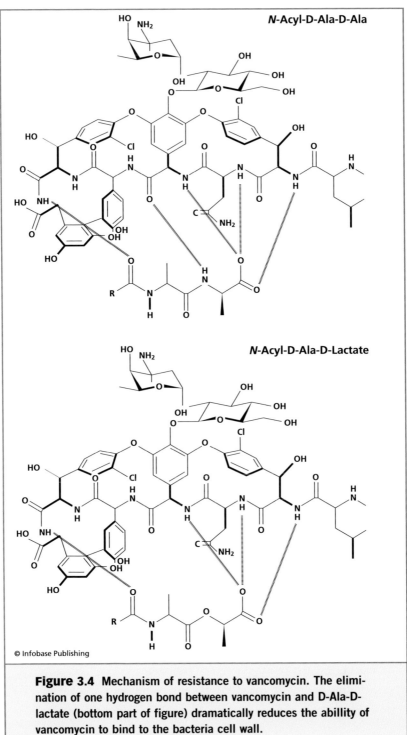

Figure 3.4 Mechanism of resistance to vancomycin. The elimination of one hydrogen bond between vancomycin and D-Ala-D-lactate (bottom part of figure) dramatically reduces the abillity of vancomycin to bind to the bacteria cell wall.

pumps have been found in a number of other bacteria. A membrane protein in *S. aureus*, for example, is involved in pumping out ciprofloxacin and related drugs, along with chloramphenicol.

TARGET OR SUBSTRATE OVERPRODUCTION

In the case of sulfonamides, one resistance mechanism involves the massive overproduction of the enzyme substrate (in this case, PABA, the starting point for the chemical reaction catalyzed by the enzyme; see Figure 2.7). Recall that sulfonamides mimic PABA, so an overabundance of this chemical means the antibiotics will have difficulty reaching their target. So much PABA will be available that the enzyme will likely always have PABA in its active site, the same location targeted by the antibiotic.

Trimethoprim resistance often results from overproduction of the enzyme (called dihydrofolate reductase, DHFR) targeted by the antibiotic. In most of these cases, the **promoter** (a DNA sequence required for the cell to make RNA) has been altered, allowing more efficient transcription of the DHFR gene. This, in turn, leads to more DHFR protein being produced; so much, in fact, that some of it will be active, even in the presence of the antibiotic, because not enough antibiotic is present inside the cell to bind to and inactivate each enzyme molecule.

REDUCED PERMEABILITY

Bacteria need to get nutrients from their environment and to excrete waste products back to the environment. The pores that bacterial cells use for this import-export trade are often the portals for antibiotic entry into cells. One generalized resistance strategy is for bacteria to make proteins that form smaller pores, thereby excluding many of these antibiotics.

This system is particularly common in Gram-negative bacteria, which have the potential to regulate the import of antibiotics at both their inner and outer membranes. For example, *P. aeruginosa* is innately resistant to many antibiotics, in part, because it has the ability to produce pores (composed of proteins called **porins**) that prevent the passage of many antibiotics. Similarly, the highly virulent *E. coli* O157:H7 strain is intrinsically resistant to several antibiotics including streptomycin, sulfonamides, and tetracyclines. This resistance appears to be due, at least in part, to the production of outer-membrane pores that restrict these antibiotics from entering the cell.

MODIFICATION OF ENZYMES THAT ACTIVATE THE ANTIBIOTIC

Most antibiotics are active against bacteria in the form supplied by the pharmacy. However, several antibiotics are prescribed in an initially inactive form. They specifically target only the bacteria capable of activating them. One example is the drug pyrazinamide, an antibiotic used to treat tuberculosis. This drug must be converted to a different compound (pyrazinoic acid) in order to become active. *Mycobacterium tuberculosis* possesses an enzyme that catalyzes this conversion; *M. tuberculosis* also lacks an efficient means of removing this activated antibiotic from the cell. Therefore mutations in the enzyme that converts pyranzinamide to pyrazinoic acid interfere with activation and confer resistance to this drug.

Isoniazid is another antituberculosis drug that requires activation. In this case, the drug passively diffuses into cells and is chemically transformed by an enzyme called KatG. This enzyme is not found in human cells, so this activation occurs only in mycobacteria. Once activated, the antibiotic blocks a key step in mycobacterial cell-wall synthesis. Resistance to isoniazid can occur in several ways, including mutation in the gene that encodes that KatG enzyme. The mutated enzyme cannot convert the antibiotic to its active form, so the bacterium becomes resistant.

A final example of resistance due to mutation in an antibiotic-activating enzyme comes from the drug metronidazole, which is frequently used to treat anaerobic bacterial infections, and stomach ulcers caused by *Helicobacter pylori*. An enzyme, common in bacteria that grow without oxygen, activates this antibiotic. Once activated, the antibiotic attacks bacterial DNA, leading to the death of the cell. Resistance to metronidazole has been associated with a reduction in the amount of activating enzyme produced by the microbe.

"HIDING" THE ANTIBIOTIC TARGET

A recently discovered resistance mechanism is the temporary occlusion of the target of the antibiotic. Drugs like ciprofloxacin and related antibiotics bind to bacterial DNA topoisomerases. In some cases of *M. tuberculosis,* resistance to these antibiotics is due to the presence of another protein that hides the target— the active site of DNA topoisomerase. This resistance protein chemically resembles the shape and size of a portion of a DNA molecule, the normal binding substrate for topoisomerases. Consequently, when DNA topoisomerase binds to this protein, it prevents the antibiotic from reaching and inactivating the Topoisomerase.

ANTIBIOTIC RESISTANCE TESTING

Determining a pathogen's spectrum of resistance to antibiotics is often a critical component in successfully treating bacterial infections. There are several methods for doing this. Two methods involve diffusion of antibiotics into an **agar medium** (agar is a compound that is used to solidify nutrients required for bacterial growth). In one of these methods, called the **disc diffusion** or **Kirby-Bauer method**, the antibiotics are impregnated into paper discs. The discs are then placed onto an agar medium, on which the pathogen is **plated** (plating means spreading the bacteria over the surface of an agar medium). As the pathogen replicates, the antibiotic diffuses into the medium. Because of diffusion, the concentration of antibiotics in the medium is lower further from the disc. The next day, the laboratory technician measures the sizes of the zones around the discs. The larger the zones, the more sensitive the bacteria are to the antibiotic.

A related method, the E-test®, uses a strip containing varying concentrations of an antibiotic. Bacteria are plated to agar media, and the strip is placed on top. The point at which bacteria grow right up to the strip indicates the minimum concentration of the antibiotic required to inhibit growth.

Another method for antibiotic resistance testing involves growing the pathogen in different concentrations of an antibiotic, and determining the minimum concentration required to inhibit growth. Most testing currently uses a microbroth dilution format, in which bacteria are inoculated in small wells of a plastic plate containing different concentrations of an antibiotic. One commonly used product is the MicroScan® system, which includes different types of plates for different types of bacteria.

With this particular diagnostic testing method, the antibiotics and dried medium are in the bottom of the well. A known amount of water and bacteria are used to rehydrate the medium and the antibiotic, and then the plastic tray is incubated overnight. The minimum concentration of antibiotic that inhibits growth in a well is used to determine whether this bacterial strain is resistant or susceptible to the antibiotic. This microbroth dilution method has a number of advantages over other methods of antibiotic susceptibility testing. It allows for the simultaneous testing of a large number of antibiotics, and the reading of plates can be automated.

Genetic methods for antibiotic resistance testing are also being developed. Some bacteria, like *M. tuberculosis*, are slow growing and take 10 days or more to give a positive or negative test with the antibiotic resistance testing methods described above. Genetic methods can overcome that limitation by potentially allowing for tests of antibiotic resistance directly on specimens taken from a patient. In these methods, the bacterium is isolated, DNA from the pathogen is liberated from the cell, and the lab worker determines whether a resistance gene or genes are present, typically using the **polymerase chain reaction** (PCR; the Polymerase Chain Reaction is a technique for making many copies of a single segment of DNA [like a resistance gene; see Figure 3.6]). If a specific resistance gene can

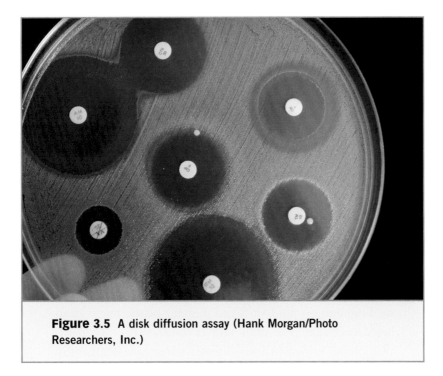

Figure 3.5 A disk diffusion assay (Hank Morgan/Photo Researchers, Inc.)

be amplified from a pathogen using PCR, it indicates that the pathogen is likely resistant to a particular antibiotic. This method is still being refined, but it may be one road to more rapid antibiotic resistance testing. The goal is to develop testing methods that are so fast that a physician can prescribe the appropriate antibiotic, based on resistance analysis, before the patient leaves the office.

REGULATION OF ANTIBIOTIC RESISTANCE

One frequently overlooked aspect of antibiotic resistance is the mechanisms by which antibiotic resistance genes are regulated. Bacteria are finely tuned reproductive machines, and the mutations that lead to antibiotic resistance often are expensive for the cell because they slow growth, make metabolism less efficient, and cause other negative effects. Therefore, in many cases, resistance is expressed only in the presence of the antibiotic. In many cases, the mechanisms for regulation of antibiotic resistance are quite elaborate.

One of the best-studied examples of the regulation of antibiotic resistance is the regulation of a gene that encodes a pump that removes tetracycline from the cell. When the pump is present, the cell is resistant to tetracycline, but it also becomes less efficient at conserving energy. Therefore, the pump is only produced when tetracycline is present in the cell. How is this achieved? If tetracycline is absent, a protein (called a **repressor**) binds the DNA next to the tetracycline resistance gene. This prevents activation (transcription) of the resistance gene, and keeps the protein pump from being made. If tetracycline is present, though, tetracycline binds to the tetracycline repressor and changes the repressor's shape so it can no longer bind to the DNA near the tetracycline resistance gene. Consequently, the tetracycline resistance gene is activated, and the tetracycline resistance protein is produced. When tetracycline levels drop low enough, the tetracycline repressor can again bind to the DNA and keep the resistance protein from being made (see Figure 3.7).

As another example, some erythromycin-resistant bacteria contain a gene required for adding a methyl group (CH_3) to the ribosomal RNA. This modification protects the cell from the antibiotic, but it can also decrease the efficiency of protein synthesis. Therefore, the cell only activates this resistance mechanism in the presence of erythromycin. How is this done? When this gene is transcribed into a messenger RNA (mRNA), the portion of the RNA before the gene has the potential to form stem-loop structures. One set of stems and loops allows the gene to be translated into a protein, thereby making the cell resistant to the antibiotic. The alternate set of stems and loops forms an inhibitory configuration that prevents this resistance protein from being made, thereby keeping the cell susceptible to the antibiotic (but more efficient at making proteins).

What determines whether the activating or inhibiting structures form? The answer, in short, is whether ribosomes

Copying DNA in the Test Tube:
the Polymerase Chain Reaction (PCR)

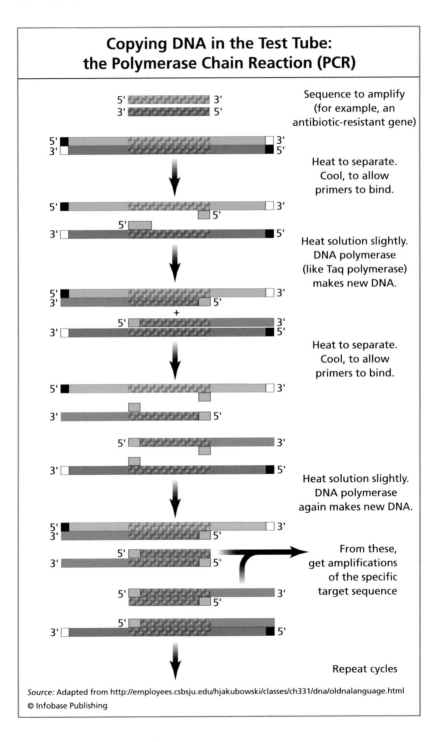

Sequence to amplify (for example, an antibiotic-resistant gene)

Heat to separate. Cool, to allow primers to bind.

Heat solution slightly. DNA polymerase (like Taq polymerase) makes new DNA.

Heat to separate. Cool, to allow primers to bind.

Heat solution slightly. DNA polymerase again makes new DNA.

From these, get amplifications of the specific target sequence

Repeat cycles

Source: Adapted from http://employees.csbsju.edu/hjakubowski/classes/ch331/dna/oldnalanguage.html
© Infobase Publishing

are having trouble doing their job. If erythromycin is starting to get into the cell, some ribosomes will not be able to work efficiently. If that is the case, they will stall on first stem-loop structure, causing the mRNA to be active and allowing the mRNA to be translated by an as-yet unaffected ribosome. In contrast, if no erythromycin is present, the ribosome will not stall and the stem-loop will form an inhibitory configuration, preventing the resistance protein from being made, and keeping the cell sensitive to the drug.

The regulation of *S. aureus* resistance to penicillin and related antibiotics has recently become understood. In *S. aureus*, two main resistance mechanisms come into play. Resistant strains contain penicillin-degrading enzymes called ß-lactamases. In addition, in strains resistant to methicillin, an alternate cell wall enzyme is produced, which doesn't bind penicillin antibiotics.

Production of ß-lactamases is turned off in the absence of penicillin and related antibiotics. However, when penicillin is present, it binds to a protein "antenna" on the surface of the bacterial cell, a protein capable of recognizing small amounts of penicillin in the environment. Once penicillin binds, it causes the internal part of this protein to cut itself in half. This fragment of the protein is now free to travel around the cell, and when it runs into another protein (the repressor) it chops the repressor in half. This repressor normally binds to the DNA near the ß-lactamase gene, preventing transcription. When the cleaved protein attaches to the repressor, the repressor is

Figure 3.6 (left) Polymerase chain reaction (PCR), a chemical reaction for copying a specific DNA in a test tube. If that specific DNA is an antibiotic resistance gene, the PCR can be used to rapidly determine if a bacterial strain is resistant to a specific antibiotic, or a group of antibiotics. In the figure, a primer is a short, single-stranded DNA molecule that binds specifically to only that one region of the bacterium's genome. As the name suggests, the primer is the place where a DNA polymerase enzyme starts making DNA.

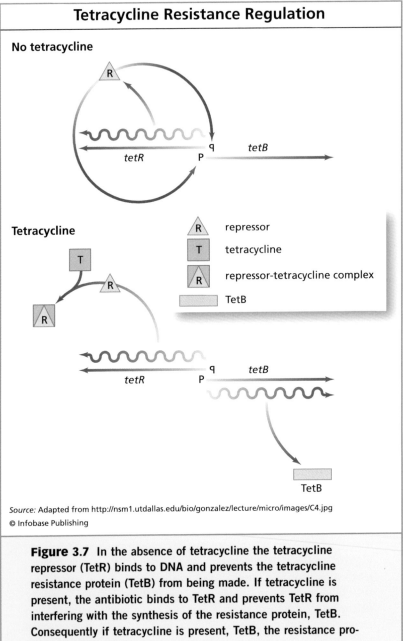

Tetracycline Resistance Regulation

No tetracycline

Tetracycline

R   repressor

T   tetracycline

R   repressor-tetracycline complex

      TetB

TetB

Source: Adapted from http://nsm1.utdallas.edu/bio/gonzalez/lecture/micro/images/C4.jpg
© Infobase Publishing

Figure 3.7 In the absence of tetracycline the tetracycline repressor (TetR) binds to DNA and prevents the tetracycline resistance protein (TetB) from being made. If tetracycline is present, the antibiotic binds to TetR and prevents TetR from interfering with the synthesis of the resistance protein, TetB. Consequently if tetracycline is present, TetB, the resistance protein, is produced.

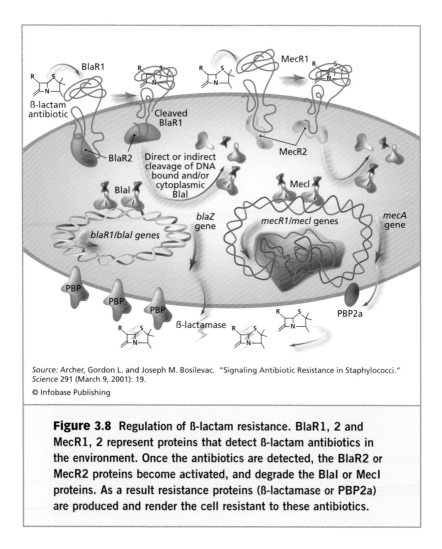

Source: Archer, Gordon L. and Joseph M. Bosilevac. "Signaling Antibiotic Resistance in Staphylococci." *Science* 291 (March 9, 2001): 19.
© Infobase Publishing

Figure 3.8 Regulation of ß-lactam resistance. BlaR1, 2 and MecR1, 2 represent proteins that detect ß-lactam antibiotics in the environment. Once the antibiotics are detected, the BlaR2 or MecR2 proteins become activated, and degrade the BlaI or MecI proteins. As a result resistance proteins (ß-lactamase or PBP2a) are produced and render the cell resistant to these antibiotics.

destroyed. This then allows the ß-lactamase gene to be transcribed, and the ß-lactamase protein to be produced (Figure 3.8).

Similarly, the cell wall enzyme, which is resistant to antibiotic binding, is not expressed in the absence of penicillin and related antibiotics. In the same way, when an antibiotic binds to a protein antenna, the intracellular part of that protein is cut off. That protein fragment travels around the cell, where it

Table 3.1 Summary of resistance for different antibiotics.

Antibiotic class (example)	Resistance Mechanism
Aminoglycosides (Streptomycin)	Antibiotic modification, Target site modification
Cephalosporins (Ceftazidime)	Antibiotic modification, Efflux (pumping out of the cell), Target site modification
Chloramphenicol	Antibiotic modification, Efflux
Glycopeptides (Vancomycin)	Target site modification
Lincosamides (Clindamycin)	Antibiotic modification, Target site modification, Efflux
Macrolides (Erythromycin)	Antibiotic modification, Efflux
Penicillins (Ampicillin)	Antibiotic modification, Efflux, Target site modification
Oxazolidinones (Linezolid)	Target site modification
Quinolones (Ciprofloxacin)	Efflux, Reduced permeability, Target site hidden, Target site modification
Rifamycins (Rifampin)	Target site modification
Streptogramins (Synercid)	Antibiotic modification, Target site modification
Sulfonamides (Sulfamethoxazole)	Efflux, Overproduction of substrate, Overproduction of target enzyme, Reduced permeability, Target site modification
Tetracyclines (Doxycycline)	Efflux, Target site hidden

encounters a repressor protein. This results in the destruction of the repressor protein, leading to production of the resistant cell wall enzyme (Figure 3.8).

These antibiotic resistance regulatory circuits are being explored as important targets for antibiotics. If the circuit could be blocked by an antibiotic, that could prevent antibiotic resistance from being expressed. Alternatively, if antibiotics are

WHERE DO ANTIBIOTIC RESISTANCE GENES COME FROM?

There are many possible origins for different antibiotic resistance genes. Some resistance genes are simply mutated versions of normal genes that retain their original function, but are no longer affected by antibiotics. One example would be proteins in bacteria that are involved in cell wall synthesis. In some cases, mutations in these genes allow them to produce proteins that still assist in cell wall synthesis yet prevent antibiotics from inactivating them. In some bacteria, a mutation in one of these genes can lead to high-level resistance to penicillin and related drugs. In other bacteria (like *S.pneumoniae*), mutations occurred in five different proteins before high-level penicillin resistance developed.

Another likely origin for some antibiotic resistance genes are mutations in genes that originally produced a protein involved in normal metabolism. Mutations in these genes have led to the production of proteins that cause antibiotic resistance. An example would be cell wall synthesis enzymes that have become adapted for attacking antibiotics.

One controversial theory suggests that a possible origin of some antibiotic resistance genes is the bacteria and fungi that produce antibiotics. Antibiotic producers must be antibiotic resistant to survive. Many bacteria are capable of exchanging genetic information, and it is possible this has happened with antibiotic producers inadvertently transferring resistance genes to other bacteria.

developed that don't trigger the signaling mechanism, the organism will remain susceptible, even though it carries the resistance genes in its genome. For example, some forms of inducible resistance to vancomycin are not activated when bacteria are exposed to a related drug, teicoplanin.

4

Causes of Antibiotic Resistance

In 1998 a young boy, who lived on a ranch in Nebraska, developed intense abdominal pain and a high fever. He was hospitalized and had his appendix removed. A review of his medical records revealed that, several weeks before the surgery, he had taken antibiotics to treat a sinus infection. Immediately before the surgery, he was again treated with antibiotics to reduce the risk of infection in the incision. In his case, the multiple doses of antibiotics probably killed important normal bacteria in his intestines, increasing his susceptibility to other infections. Following the surgery, he developed diarrhea, caused by a microbe called *Salmonella enterica*. This particular strain was resistant to a wide range of antibiotics including ampicillin, aztreonam, cefoxitin, ceftriaxone, cephalothin, chloramphenicol, gentamicin, kanamycin, sulfamethsoxizole, streptomycin, tetracycline, and tobramycin. Fortunately, the boy's immune system was able to fight the infection, and he recovered. Further investigation revealed that cattle on his ranch and neighboring ranches were treated for *Salmonella* infections a month before he became infected. A study of genetic "fingerprints" of the microbes indicated that the boy likely acquired the antibiotic-resistant bacteria from cattle either on his ranch or a neighboring ranch.[9] This incident supported the idea that antibiotic-resistant bacteria from animals can cause disease in humans.

The fundamental cause of antibiotic resistance is a strong selective pressure favoring resistant bacteria in the presence of the drugs. Resistant bacteria survive an otherwise lethal onslaught of an antibiotic, which places a premium on developing resistance. Since bacteria reproduce so

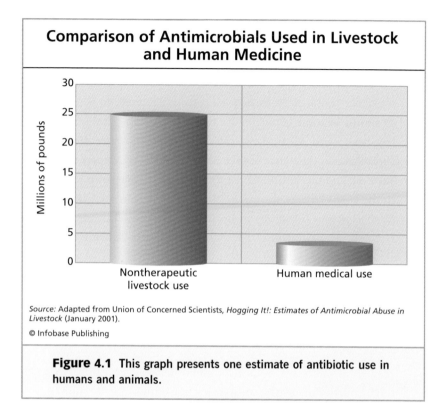

Figure 4.1 This graph presents one estimate of antibiotic use in humans and animals.

quickly, a single resistant bacterium can become millions of resistant bacteria in hours. In the absence of an antibiotic these mutant, resistant bacteria are often initially at a disadvantage compared to normal bacteria, since the mutations often slow the rate of bacterial reproduction. Additional mutations often occur, however, which compensate for the disadvantage. In addition, resistance often develops when a bacterium acquires a resistance gene from another microbe, and in that case, there is little selective disadvantage to the now-resistant microbe.

Added to the problem of rapid bacterial multiplication is the selective pressure exerted by the huge volume of antibiotics used in human medicine and agriculture. Estimates range from 27 to 50 million pounds of antibiotics used per year in the United States.[10] Some health authorities feel that much of that antibiotic usage is inappropriate and is increasingly leading to disease transmission in animals and humans, as highlighted in the opening story of this chapter.

Recent data indicates the extent of the growing antibiotic-resistance problem. In *Escherichia coli*, for example, 80 percent of strains in some countries are resistant to ampicillin, which has been used to treat *E. coli* infections since the 1960s. Ciprofloxacin resistance is over 30 percent in some species of bacteria, and this antibiotic has only been available since 1987. In the United States, during 1999–2000, 43 percent of *Staphylococcus aureus* infections in hospitals were caused by strains resistant to methicillin. These infections are difficult and expensive to treat.[11]

Antibiotics are widely used to treat disease both in humans and animals. Antibiotics are also widely used to promote growth in animals. Estimates of the proportion of antibiotics used in humans and animals vary widely (Figure 4.1, 4.2), but it is clear that millions of pounds of these drugs are used each year. That's about 3 million pounds. Between one-third to three-fourths of all the antibiotics consumed are for nontherapeutic uses in animals. Because a sizeable portion of many antibiotics is excreted unaltered by people and animals, a large quantity of antibiotics enters sewage treatment facilities, which they often leave unaltered, and ultimately wind up in lakes and rivers. Therefore a vast number of bacteria are exposed to a huge volume of antibiotics each year.

There are several lines of evidence suggesting that bacteria in the environment may develop resistance as a result of antibiotic exposure. First, antibiotics are widespread in the environment. A recent study conducted by the U.S. Geological Survey found that 22 percent of streams and rivers sampled contained detectable amounts of antibiotics.[12] Even low levels of antibiotic exposure may help bacteria develop resistance, so this finding concerns many health experts. Second, two recent reports from Europe shed some light on the connection

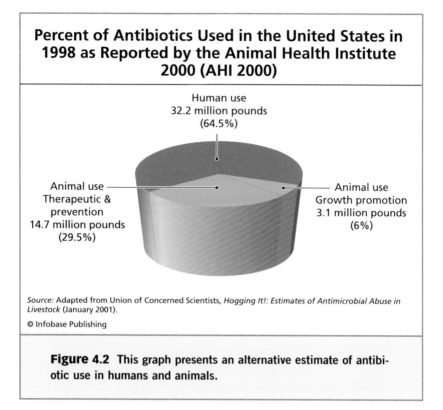

Percent of Antibiotics Used in the United States in 1998 as Reported by the Animal Health Institute 2000 (AHI 2000)

Human use
32.2 million pounds
(64.5%)

Animal use
Therapeutic &
prevention
14.7 million pounds
(29.5%)

Animal use
Growth promotion
3.1 million pounds
(6%)

Source: Adapted from Union of Concerned Scientists, *Hogging It!: Estimates of Antimicrobial Abuse in Livestock* (January 2001).

© Infobase Publishing

Figure 4.2 This graph presents an alternative estimate of antibiotic use in humans and animals.

between antibiotic exposure and resistance. One report found that wild mice and other rodents from two woodland habitats in England harbored a large population of antibiotic-resistant bacteria. For example, more than 90 percent of the intestinal bacteria the researchers studied were resistant to amoxycillin.[13] In contrast, a study of the intestinal bacteria from several different mammals from wilderness areas in Finland showed low levels of antibiotic resistance.[14] This suggests that animals living in closer proximity to humans are more likely to harbor antibiotic-resistant bacteria, presumably due to greater exposure to antibiotics in the environment.

Bacteria in even closer proximity to humans are those that inhabit the animals or animal products destined to wind up in grocery stores. As one example of the threat, scientists discovered a common bacterium in unpasteurized cheese that contained genes conferring resistance to streptomycin, tetracycline, chloramphenicol, and erythromycin. The surprising part of this study was that DNA sequence analysis indicated that this nonpathogenic, or non–disease-causing, microbe (*Lactococcus lactis*) had acquired resistance genes from a variety of human pathogens including *Streptococcus pyogenes, S. aureus,* and *Listeria moncytogenes.* [15]   This suggests that resistance genes can be readily transferred from one bacterium to another either inside an animal or during food processing. Other recent studies indicate that some bacteria resistant to multiple drugs can be transmitted from farm animals to humans, potentially leading to serious illness.

The most controversial use of antibiotics in agriculture is for the promotion of growth in animals. For reasons scientists don't fully understand, adding low doses of antibiotics to animal feed can increase the growth rate in animals by 4 to 5 percent. For farmers struggling financially, this increase can make the difference between survival and bankruptcy. It can also lower food prices for consumers. Yet, because this practice may make some human infections more difficult to treat, debate continues over balancing those competing interests.

Even in less controversial situations, the use of antibiotics to treat diseases in animals can still be a difficult balancing act. One example is the use of fluoroquinolone antibiotics in poultry. These are chemically related to important human antibiotics, including ciprofloxacin. In 1996 the U.S. Food and Drug Administration (FDA) approved the use of fluorquinolone antibiotics for treating respiratory infections in chickens. However, by 2000 the FDA became concerned about the rising levels of antibiotic resistance in *Campylobacter jejuni,* which can be transmitted from chickens to humans who eat chicken. In 2005 the use of these antibiotics to treat chickens was banned in the United States.

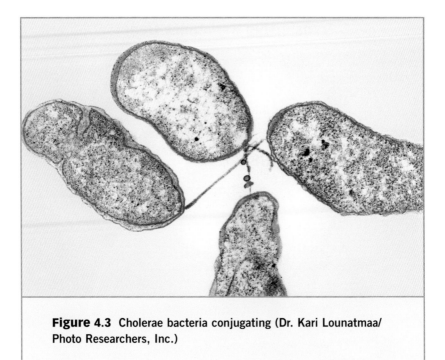

Figure 4.3 Cholerae bacteria conjugating (Dr. Kari Lounatmaa/ Photo Researchers, Inc.)

In spite of their presence in the environment and use in agriculture, it is likely that resistance in most pathogens develops as a result of antibiotic exposure in or around humans. Selection pressure is one factor. For example, exposure to antibiotics can lead to selection for resistant microbes in the intestines and other locations in our bodies. This normal intestinal flora can then pass antibiotic resistance genes to pathogenic microbes.

The widespread use of antibiotics can lead to the widespread development of antibiotic resistance. But if each individual bacterial strain had to start from scratch in developing resistance, it would take a long time for antibiotic resistance to become a major health problem. The transfer of antibiotic resistance genes between different strains or species of bacteria speeds up this process.

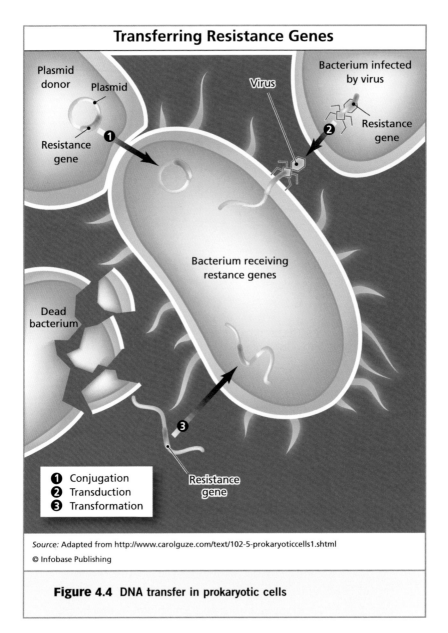

Transferring Resistance Genes

Plasmid donor

Plasmid

Resistance gene

❶

Virus

Bacterium infected by virus

❷

Resistance gene

Bacterium receiving restance genes

Dead bacterium

❸

Resistance gene

❶ Conjugation
❷ Transduction
❸ Transformation

Source: Adapted from http://www.carolguze.com/text/102-5-prokaryoticcells1.shtml
© Infobase Publishing

Figure 4.4 DNA transfer in prokaryotic cells

Antibiotic resistance genes are transferred through several mechanisms: **transformation**, **conjugation**, or **transduction** (Figure 4.3, 4.4). Transformation involves the uptake of DNA

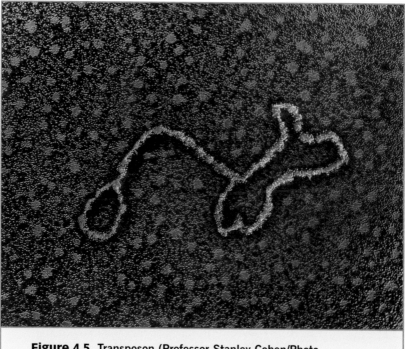

Figure 4.5 Transposon (Professor Stanley Cohen/Photo Researchers, Inc.)

from the liquid surrounding the microbe. Bacterial pathogens like *Streptococcus pneumoniae* have this ability. If the DNA absorbed contains a resistance gene, the bacteria may be able to incorporate it into their genome and lose their susceptibility to an antibiotic.

The process of conjugation can be considered the bacterial equivalent of sex (Figure 4.3). During this process, genetic material is transferred from a donor bacterium to a recipient bacterium. Specifically, circular DNA molecules, called **plasmids**, are transferred. These plasmids frequently contain antibiotic resistance genes, causing the bacterial recipient to lose susceptibility to an antibiotic. Other genetic elements, called **transposons** (Figure 4.5), have the ability to "jump" from one site of a chromosome to another location, and ultimately, from one strain of bacteria to another. These genetic elements also frequently contain antibiotic resistance genes. Finally, **integrons** represent perhaps the most frightening example of the potential for these gene-transfer mechanisms to create a "Superbug." Integrons are a type of transposon that contains a series of antibiotic resistance genes. These integrons have the ability to jump into new genomes, or into conjugative plasmids, allowing them to disseminate widely.

Transduction is another method of DNA transfer. Normally bacteriophages (bacterial viruses) destroy bacterial cells.

HIV AND RESISTANCE TO ANTIVIRAL AGENTS

Drug resistance is not restricted to bacteria and has become a problem in treating many infections, including those caused by viruses. The Human Immunodeficiency Virus (HIV), the causative agent of AIDS, rapidly becomes resistant to antiviral agents. This is due, at least in part, to the very sloppy method the virus uses to copy its genetic information. The viral enzyme responsible for this process is very error-prone, resulting in an average of one mutation per virus per generation. Since an infected individual typically harbors billions or perhaps trillions of HIV viruses, there is a huge pool of mutant viruses available for selection. If any of these mutations result in resistance to an antiviral drug, that mutant viral strain will rapidly become predominant. This has been observed in the course of infections; in people treated with a single anti-HIV drug, like Zidovudine (AZT), resistance rapidly develops. This is one of the reasons that the current treatment for HIV infection is a cocktail containing three or four different antiviral agents. If the drugs are taken properly, it is improbable a virus will develop resistance to all three or four drugs simultaneously.

In this case, the bacteriophages instead transfer DNA from one bacterium to another. Again, the potential exists for transduction to lead to resistance gene transfer.

5

Consequences of Antibiotic Resistance

"The History of Medicine"[16]

2000 B.C.	– Here, eat this root
1000 A.D.	– That root is heathen. Here, say this prayer.
1850 A.D.	– That prayer is superstition. Here, drink this potion.
1920 A.D.	– That potion is snake oil. Here, swallow this pill.
1945 A.D.	– That pill is ineffective. Here, take this penicillin.
1955 A.D.	– Oops....bugs mutated. Here, take this tetracycline.
1960–1999	– 39 more "oops"...Here, take this more powerful antibiotic.
2000 A.D.	– The bugs have won! Here, eat this root."

Anonymous

Staphylococcus aureus has long been a major human pathogen. Initially, penicillin was an effective treatment, but penicillin-resistant strains rapidly developed. This drove the search for new antibiotics, such as methicillin, which initially were effective against penicillin-resistant *S. aureus*. Methicillin resistance eventually developed as well, leaving the antibiotic vancomycin as the last line of defense against this tenacious microbe. In Michigan in July 2002, doctors reported the first case of vancomycin-resistant *S. aureus*.[17] This ominous development shows the difficulty of staying ahead of microbes in the antibiotic resistance race. Several new antibiotics have recently become available for treating multiple antibiotic-resistant *S. aureus*, but it may be only a matter of time before widespread resistance to these drugs develops as well.

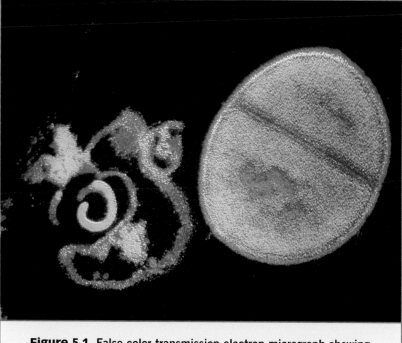

Figure 5.1 False-color transmission electron micrograph showing the effect of an antibiotic on the bacterium *Staphylococcus aureus*. On the left are the remains of a bacterium destroyed by lysis (bursting); the bacterium at right is, as yet, undamaged and is in the process of dividing. (CNRI/Photo Researchers, Inc.)

For individuals, antibiotic-resistant microbes are a major problem. People infected with an antibiotic-resistant microbe are more likely to be hospitalized compared to a person infected with a strain of the same microbe that is not antibiotic resistant. In addition, infections with resistant microbes lead to longer hospital stays and increase the risk of dying due to the infection. The direct economic costs from an infection with antibiotic-resistant bacteria can be substantial. For example, infections of hospitalized patients with antibiotic-resistant *Pseudomonas aeruginosa* cost an average of $7,340 more than stays for patients infected with antibiotic-sensitive strains.

Hospital patients infected with methicillin-resistant *S. aureus* had a significantly higher risk of death, and their hospital stays cost an average of $4,000 more than those of patients infected with susceptible strains of *S. aureus*. The cost of treatment for multi–drug-resistant tuberculosis can be $180,000 or more, whereas the cost for treating drug-sensitive tuberculosis can be as low as $2,000. Taking into account lost wages and other factors, the overall costs associated with antibiotic-resistant bacteria are estimated to be $4 to $5 billion per year in the United States.

Other losses are harder to quantify. The National Institutes of Health have estimated that 90,000 people die each year in the United States as a result of infections with antibiotic-resistant bacteria. More than two million people develop infections while hospitalized, and nearly three-fourths of those infections are caused by bacteria resistant to at least one common antibiotic.[18] It's impossible to quantify the personal losses associated with individual deaths due to antibiotic-resistant bacteria.

There are also issues with quality of life. Antibiotic resistance translates into a higher prevalence of infection, and therefore, more people suffer the pain and trauma associated with a disease. One example is gonorrhea, once easily remedied with penicillin and tetracyclines but now increasingly difficult to treat in many parts of the world. Many strains of this bacterium have become resistant to those inexpensive drugs and frequently must be treated with more expensive medicines, like azithromycin and ciprofloxacin. In women, untreated gonorrhea can result in lifelong complications, such as pelvic inflammatory disease, which can cause potentially fatal ectopic pregnancies and infertility.

Another consequence of widespread antibiotic resistance is loss of confidence in the health care system. Some observers think much of the public's high regard for modern medicine is based on the rapid cures of otherwise lethal infections through administration of antibiotic treatments.[8] Widespread

WHY DO SOME SPECIES OF BACTERIA REMAIN SENSITIVE TO ANTIBIOTICS?

For all the concern about antibiotic resistance, it is interesting to note that some species of bacteria have not yet developed resistance to common antibiotics, like penicillin. One striking example is *Streptococcus pyogenes*, the cause of Strep throat, rheumatic fever, and other ailments. This microbe is still universally susceptible to penicillin even though this drug has been used for more than 60 years to treat Strep throat. Why has this organism failed to evolve resistance to this drug when other bacteria, like *Staphylococcus aureus*, developed widespread resistance in less than a decade, and others, like *Streptococcus pneumoniae*, became resistant after several decades? The answer is not clear, but one factor may be the inability of *S. pyogenes* to acquire or use antibiotic resistance genes from other microbes. Another factor may be a requirement for the mutation of multiple genes. In *S. pneumoniae*, for example, multiple gene mutations are required for resistance to penicillin. That is a much more improbable event than a single gene mutation. *S. pyogenes* may require multiple mutations to become penicillin resistant, and the conditions may not yet have been right for that degree of selection. However, not everything is bright in this example. There has been an increase in recent years in the prevalence of macrolide resistance (e.g., erythromycin) in *S. pyogenes*, indicating that antibiotic resistance may yet be a significant problem with this organism.

In some other cases, because of the nature of disease transmission, antibiotic resistance hasn't developed and is unlikely to develop. The bacterium that causes Lyme disease, *Borrelia burgdorferi*, is transmitted from ticks to humans. Since this disease doesn't spread from person to person, resistant bacteria that may develop during antibiotic treatment won't be transmitted to another human. In addition, the bacteria in ticks shouldn't develop resistance because they are not exposed to antibiotics.

antibiotic resistance leading to a greater number of untreatable infections might diminish confidence in the medical system. This could lead to, among other things, increased use of unorthodox, unapproved, ineffective treatments, although that scenario is probably far off.

6

The Most Dangerous Antibiotic- Resistant Bacteria

"If the importance of a disease for mankind is measured from the number of fatalities due to it, then tuberculosis must be considered much more important than those most feared infectious diseases, plague, cholera, and the like. Statistics have shown that 1/7th of all humans die of tuberculosis."[19]

Robert Koch, 1882

ANTIBIOTIC-RESISTANT *MYCOBACTERIUM TUBERCULOSIS* INFECTIONS

Tuberculosis (TB) is still a major problem for humanity. Tuberculosis kills nearly two million people per year, and approximately one-third of the world's population (about two billion people) are infected with the bacterium that causes this disease. Symptoms of tuberculosis are quite varied, depending on which organs are infected. However, most cases of tuberculosis show symptoms, at least initially, due to infection in the lungs, or pulmonary tuberculosis. Common symptoms of this include cough and chest pain. Other more generalized symptoms include fever and weight loss. Infection normally occurs when a person inhales *Mycobacterium tuberculosis* that has been expelled from a person with the disease.

Mycobacterium tuberculosis infections provided some of the first examples of clinical antibiotic resistance. Initially, streptomycin was the only antibiotic available to treat tuberculosis. In patients treated with this single drug, up to 40 percent harbored streptomycin-resistant M. tuberculosis within a year after the start of drug therapy.[20] The numbers help explain this; a mutation leading to streptomycin resistance occurs about once in every 100 million times M. tuberculosis divides; a person infected with M. tuberculosis may harbor approximately one billion bacteria. Therefore, by chance, as many as 10 of these bacteria will be resistant to the drug. These bacteria have a selective advantage over streptomycin-sensitive bacteria so that they will continue to grow and eventually become predominant.

In subsequent years, a number of other effective anti-tuberculosis drugs were developed. This led to the simultaneous administration of multiple antibiotics as the standard treatment for tuberculosis. These drugs included rifampin, isoniazid, ethambutol, and pyrazinamide. When taken as recommended, resistance is extremely unlikely to develop; if the frequency of drug-resistant mutations for each antibiotic was one in a million, the frequency of simultaneous resistance to all three antibiotics would be 1 in a quintillion (10^{18}).

Because of this multiple-antibiotic treatment regime, cases of tuberculosis declined substantially between the 1950s and the mid-1980s in industrialized countries. In other countries, however, tuberculosis remains prevalent. In Africa, for example, there are approximately three new cases per year for every 1,000 people, in contrast to a rate of approximately three new cases per year for every 100,000 people in the united States.

Multi–drug-resistant M. tuberculosis became a major public health concern when the number of tuberculosis cases shot up in the United States during the 1990s (Figure 6.1). Multi–drug-resistant tuberculosis (MDR-TB) is defined as tuberculosis caused by strains that are resistant to at least two of the front-line drugs: isoniazid, rifampin, ethambutol, and pyrazinamide. Several factors conspired for this rapid increase. One was the HIV epidemic, which resulted in a large

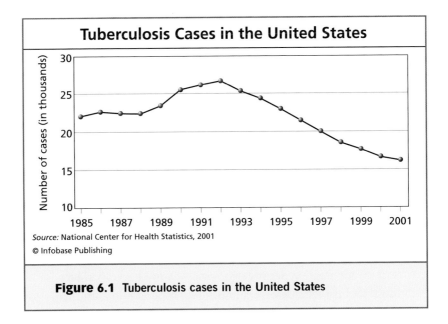

Figure 6.1 Tuberculosis cases in the United States

number of people who were more susceptible to TB. Another was the dismantling of anti-TB health services, based on the decline of TB cases following the introduction of effective antibiotics. For example, programs that verified that patients were taking their drugs appropriately were no longer in place. One consequence was that many patients didn't adhere to the months-long regime of taking anti-TB drugs; they would take one or two drugs at a time, leading bacteria to become resistant to one of the drugs. If their TB became symptomatic again and they resumed taking antibiotics, the growing resistance in the bacteria now effectively rendered the four-drug treatment a two-drug treatment or even a one-drug treatment. This led to the development of some TB strains that were resistant to three of the four front-line TB drugs.

In the United States, reestablishing the health network for Directly Observed Tuberculosis Treatment Short Course (DOTS) reversed this trend. This resulted in nearly uniform, effective TB treatment and a reduction in the number of cases of TB and multi-drug resistant TB. In several places in the world, such as parts of China, Russia, and Estonia, the incidence of MDR-TB is still greater than 10 percent of TB cases. With the rapidity of global travel, this poses a real threat for transfer of these intensely resistant strains throughout the world. The costs of treating MDR-TB and the risk of death from MDR-TB are much higher than those from infection with drug-susceptible *M. tuberculosis.* Therefore, controlling this dangerous human pathogen requires continued vigilance.

STAPHYLOCOCCUS AUREUS INFECTIONS CAUSED BY ANTIBIOTIC-RESISTANT BACTERIA

Staphylococcus aureus causes skin and tissue infections and can invade many other organs. Some strains of *S. aureus* produce toxins that cause food poisoning; other strains produce toxins that cause toxic shock syndrome. This organism commonly resides on the skin, usually not causing problems until a cut or other injury allows it to enter normally protected tissue. *S. aureus* skin infections result in the production of pimples or boils. Fever and chills may occur, along with redness and swelling at the site of infection. *S. aureus* remains an important pathogen, particularly among people who are hospitalized. For example, in the United States, between 1999 and 2000, about one percent of hospital patients had or acquired *S. aureus* infection, and nearly half of these infections were caused by strains resistant to multiple antibiotics.

Staphylococcus aureus continues to be one of the most difficult pathogens to treat because of its resistance to antibiotics. The most resistant strains have typically been found in hospitals, particularly in intensive care units, where antibiotics are extensively used. Therefore it was shocking when four young children, with no other underlying diseases, died from antibiotic-resistant *S. aureus* in 1999. One of these children, a 13-year-old girl from rural Minnesota, was taken to the hospital coughing up blood. She had difficulty breathing and

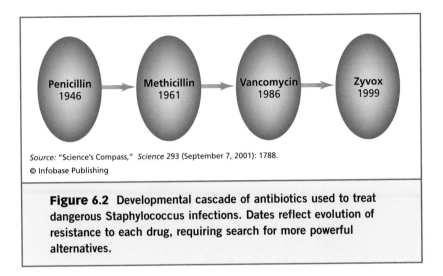

Source: "Science's Compass," Science 293 (September 7, 2001): 1788.
© Infobase Publishing

Figure 6.2 Developmental cascade of antibiotics used to treat dangerous Staphylococcus infections. Dates reflect evolution of resistance to each drug, requiring search for more powerful alternatives.

suffered from a high fever. She was initially treated with a cephalosporin antibiotic. Shortly thereafter, she went into shock, and was treated with vancomycin and a different cephalosporin antibiotic. Her breathing difficulty worsened, and she died of organ failure seven days after entering the hospital. Laboratory results indicated she had been infected with methicillin-resistant *S. aureus.*

Staphylococcus aureus is a versatile, robust human pathogen that can cause disease in nearly any organ and tissue in the body. The various *S. aureus* strains are capable of producing a witch's brew of toxins and other virulence factors, and in fact, the four strains of *S. aureus* that killed the four children in 1999 each produced at least one toxin.

The widespread availability of penicillin in the 1940s offered hope that modern medicine had defeated this human scourge. Yet by 1960, about half of *S. aureus* strains were resistant to the antibiotic. Fortunately, a new antibiotic, methicillin, could treat most of these infections. Widespread resistance to methicillin eventually developed and, by 1996, about one-third of *S. aureus* strains were no longer susceptible to this drug. This led to the widespread use of the antibiotic vancomycin to treat

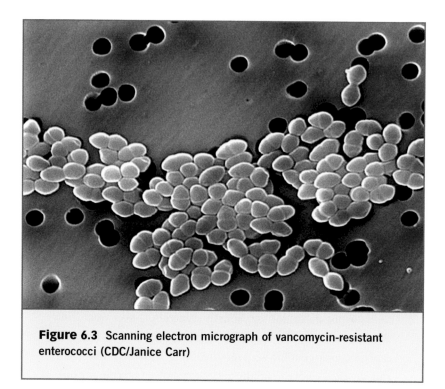

Figure 6.3 Scanning electron micrograph of vancomycin-resistant enterococci (CDC/Janice Carr)

S. aureus infections. In 2002, the first strains of *S. aureus* fully resistant to vancomycin were identified. Several new classes of antibiotics have been recently approved for use to treat multi–drug-resistant *S. aureus*. Based on past history, however, it is likely to be only a matter of time before significant resistance to these drugs develops (Figure 6.2).

ANTIBIOTIC-RESISTANT ENTEROCOCCI

Infections caused by *Enterococci* had not, until recently, been considered a significant problem. In fact, members of this genus are normal inhabitants of the human intestine and had been generally regarded as nonpathogenic. However, it has become clear that *Enterococci* (specifically *Enterococcus faecalis* and *Enterococcus faecium*) frequently cause infections in hospitalized patients and people who are immunocompromised.

Infections generally occur when these microbes enter a wound, such as a surgical wound, or colonize a medical device, like a catheter. Initially these infections were readily treated with vancomycin, but vancomycin-resistant *Enterococci* have become more common (Figure 6.3). *Enterococci* currently cause more than 200,000 infections per year in the United States, most acquired in hospitals. Antibiotic-resistant bacteria caused many of these infections. For example, in 1997, more than 50 percent of *E. faecium* infections were caused by vancomycin-resistant strains, and more than 83 percent were resistant to ampicillin. These resistant strains can cause serious, even fatal infections, particularly in individuals who are immunocompromised. The following case report illustrates this.

An elderly man with diabetes, kidney disease, and high blood pressure was admitted to a hospital in Texas, complaining of weakness in his legs. Diagnostic tests revealed he had a ruptured disk in his spinal column, which was treated with surgery. Following surgery the patient developed a fever, and cultures of his blood indicated the presence of *Enterococci* (normally the blood is sterile). The man was given vancomycin and gentamicin, and his fever diminished. Further diagnostic tests, however, revealed the apparent presence of bacteria growing on his heart valves. The man was transferred to another facility for further treatment, but he died shortly thereafter.

In addition to the problem of enterococcal infections, a major concern is the transfer of vancomycin resistance from *Enterococci* to *S. aureus*. This apparently did, in fact, happen in the first reported case of vancomycin-resistant *S. aureus* in 2002. Molecular evidence of bacterial strains isolated from the patient showed that the same genes conferring vancomycin resistance were present in both *Enterococci* and *S. aureus*. If this type of DNA transfer becomes widely established, it could herald a major problem in treating *S. aureus* infections.

ANTIBIOTIC-RESISTANT *STREPTOCOCCUS PNEUMONIAE* INFECTIONS

Streptococcus pneumoniae was a leading cause of death in the United States and many other countries in the first half of the 20th century. It is still a serious cause of disease in the United States and many other parts of the world. As the species name suggests, it causes pneumonia. This pathogen also causes many inner ear infections and can also cause meningitis and other invasive diseases. Many people naturally carry this organism in their mouths or throats; when their immune system is weakened, the pathogen can invade the lungs. In some cases, the disease is also acquired from other infected individuals.

As with staph infections, the widespread availability of penicillin dramatically reduced deaths from this pathogen. In contrast with *S. aureus*, though, widespread antibiotic resistance was slow to develop in *S. pneumoniae*. The first report of penicillin resistance in this pathogen came from Australia in 1967; the first report in the United States was in 1974.[21] However, it wasn't until the mid-1980s that resistance to penicillin became widespread, about 40 years after the antibiotic was introduced. Subsequently, the incidence of penicillin-resistant strains increased rapidly. For example, in Europe between the mid-1980s and 2003, the incidence of penicillin-resistant strains increased from near zero to about 24 percent; resistance to erythromycin and other antibiotics similarly increased from near zero to 28 percent.[22] In 1990 only four percent of *S. pneumoniae* isolates studied in the United States were not susceptible to penicillin. By 2003, 32 percent of *S. pneumoniae* infections in one U.S. study didn't respond to penicillin.[23] In another U.S. study, *S. pneumoniae* strains not susceptible to penicillin increased more than 10 percent between 1994 and 2000; resistance to erythromycin increased 16 percent during this same period.[24] In these studies, a substantial fraction of these strains were also resistant to other antibiotics.

One question regarding penicillin and *S. pneumoniae* was why it took so long for drug resistance to become common. Molecular analysis of resistant *S. pneumoniae* revealed the answer: five Penicillin Binding Proteins (PBPs), required for cell-wall synthesis, had to be mutated in order for the organism to be fully resistant to the drug. Development of resistance likely began with a mutant with a single modified PBP; this mutant could tolerate a slightly higher penicillin concentration compared to nonmutant strains. Subsequent exposure to low doses of penicillin may have selected for new strains of this mutant, which now had two PBPs that were modified; the strain was becoming resistant to the drug. This process was apparently repeated over time until all five PBPs were mutated so they no longer bound penicillin. The result is *S. pneumoniae* strains that are highly resistant to penicillin and related drugs.

SALMONELLA ENTERICA INFECTIONS RESISTANT TO ANTIBIOTIC TREATMENT

Salmonella enterica serotype typhimurum is thought to cause more than one million cases of illness per year in the United States. In most cases, symptoms include diarrhea, vomiting, fever, and abdominal cramps. For most people, these unpleasant symptoms pass fairly quickly without medical intervention. However, approximately 15,000 people in the United States are hospitalized each year following infection with this organism, and approximately 600 people die from the illness.[25] The infection is generally acquired by ingesting food contaminated with this microbe, although it can also be acquired by directly handling fecal material from infected animals.

As with many bacteria, antibiotic resistance has increased substantially over the past 20 to 30 years. In the case of *Salmonella* infections, at least some of this increase is attributed to the widespread use of antibiotics in animals. In particular, one group of *S. enterica* strains, DT104, has been notable because of its broad spectrum of antibiotic resistance. These strains are

NEW PATHOGENS GAIN A FOOTHOLD AS THEY BECOME HIGHLY ANTIBIOTIC RESISTANT

Acinetobacter baumannii and related species are found naturally on the skin of about one in four people. These organisms were once considered nonpathogenic, but it is now clear they can be an important source of infections in hospital patients. They can cause a variety of diseases including urinary tract infections and bone infections, but the majority of hospital-acquired infections caused by *Acinetobacter* species are lung infections leading to pneumonia. This organism is very hardy in the environment; it can survive dried for nearly a week, and it has the ability to grow in alkaline and acidic conditions and at a variety of temperatures. Its hardiness means it can potentially be transmitted from a variety of surfaces and patients; a recent report suggested that cell phones used by doctors and nurses can harbor the bacteria and might be a reservoir for transmission of bacteria to patients.

In terms of its medical importance, this organism is particularly noteworthy because of its resistance to a variety of antibiotics as a result of exposure to antibiotics causing selection of resistant strains. Until the 1970s, *Acinetobacter* species could be treated with a wide range of antibiotics. Currently, many *Acinetobacter* infections are nearly untreatable; some isolates are resistant to penicillins and related drugs, gentamicin and related aminoglycosides, chloramphenicol, and tetracyclines. Imipenim is one of the few antibiotics that is still effective on almost all of these strains, but increasing levels of resistance to this drug are being reported as well. Most patients who develop serious *Acinetobacter* infections are somewhat immunocompromised. However, otherwise healthy individuals who have a serious traumatic injury are also occasionally infected with this organism.

commonly resistant to ampicillin, chloramphenicol, streptomycin, sulfonamides, and tetracyclines; and some of these strains are resistant to other antibiotics as well. This strain was first reported in England in the early 1980s. It became increasingly common worldwide by the mid-1990s, and in some regions, more than 50 percent of the *S. enterica* strains isolated from patients are currently DT104.[26] Because of the wide spectrum of antibiotic resistance in this strain, relatively few antibiotics are available for treatment. The antibiotics that are potentially still available for treatment include fluoroquinolones, cephalosporins, or trimethoprim. Resistance of these strains to fluoroquinolones and trimethoprim has been reported to be more than 10 percent in some areas, indicating an increased likelihood for antibiotic treatment failures.

The following case study demonstrates the seriousness of multi–drug-resistant *Salmonella* infections:

A man was admitted to a hospital suffering from diarrhea resulting from a *Salmonella* infection. He was treated with multiple antibiotics but succumbed to the disease, dying shortly after admission to the hospital. Five weeks later, nine other people in the same hospital developed severe *Salmonella* infections, caused by the same *Salmonella* strain that killed the initial patient; two of these people died. A careful analysis of data from the hospital turned up two staff members who had apparently developed **asymptomatic** infections—they had *Salmonella* infections but showed no signs of disease. These individuals were shedding the bacteria, and appeared to have been the source of the outbreak five weeks after the first case. The institution of stringent handwashing measures prevented any additional cases.

7

Strategies to Combat Antibiotic Resistance

CASE STUDY

A woman who had a pre-existing heart condition was given the antibiotic clindamycin as a preventive measure prior to undergoing some dental work. Shortly thereafter, she developed a bacterial infection in her heart, apparently from oral bacteria that entered her bloodstream during the dental procedure. Further treatment with clindamycin was unsuccessful; but fortunately another relatively new antibiotic, linezolid, was available and was effective at treating the infection. However, as a result of the damage caused by the initial infection the woman required surgery to replace one of her heart valves.[27]

This partial success story of antibiotic treatment represents a decades-old strategy for treating resistant infections: trying a new antibiotic. Since the 1950s, the discovery and development of new antibiotics has been critical for keeping antibiotic-resistant bacteria at bay. This has continued into the 21st century with the approval of a new tetracycline-like antibiotic, Tygacil, in 2005. In the last decade, however, the pace of development of new antibiotics has slowed substantially, and this trend is likely to continue. It typically takes 10 to 15 years from discovery to drug approval for a new antibiotic to reach the market, and relatively few are in the pipeline today. Many health experts recommend a renewed focus on antibiotic development, but pharmaceutical companies find drugs developed to treat long-term chronic illness, like heart disease or diabetes, more profitable. Ironically there is some danger in curbing resistance, because it reduces the potential market for new antibiotics and lowers the likelihood that pharmaceutical companies will expend the resources to develop these drugs.

Although development of new antibiotics will likely remain critical to combating antibiotic-resistant bacteria, a number of other strategies currently in use (or in development) are becoming equally important. Preventing antibiotic resistance slams head-on into several key features of bacterial biology, such as fast growth rate, large population size, and the effect of selection on mutation prevalence. This makes thwarting antibiotic resistance a difficult challenge.

One very simple method to stop the spread of resistant microbes is better infection—control measures, particularly in medical settings. For example, patients infected with resistant pathogens could be isolated, and hospitals should enforce thorough hand washing and the use of alcohol-based hand lotions when sinks aren't readily accessible.

Another strategy is to curtail inappropriate antibiotic prescriptions. Respiratory infections, for example, are often caused by viruses, but some physicians prescribe antibiotics to treat them in part because patients sometimes demand a pill for any malady they may have. To combat this, some hospitals and clinics have instituted programs to monitor antibiotic prescriptions and withdraw inappropriately prescribed antibiotics. These programs have been unpopular among some physicians and their patients, but they indicate a growing awareness in the medical community of the seriousness of antibiotic resistance.

A related strategy is to limit antibiotic use in agriculture, an industry that consumes a substantial portion of all antibiotics. Several recent governmental decisions have addressed this. In 1997 the European Union banned the use of avoparcin, an antibiotic chemically similar to vancomycin, after several studies indicated that its use in agriculture had increased the prevalence of vancomycin-resistant bacteria in Europe. Banning this drug resulted in a rapid and substantial drop in the prevalence of vancomycin-resistant bacteria in Europe. Similarly, the U.S. Food and Drug Administration banned the use of enrofloxacin (chemically related to ciprofloxacin) in 2005. Research indicated that an important food-borne pathogen (*Campylobacter jejuni*), which can be transmitted from chickens to humans, is more likely to become resistant to these drugs following use of this related antibiotic in chickens. In 1995, the year before approval of enrofloxacin, almost no strains of *C. jejuni* were resistant to ciprofloxacin in the United States. By 2004, 20 percent or more of *C. jejuni* strains that caused infections in humans were resistant to ciprofloxacin. Most observers attributed that increase mainly to the use of enrofloxacin to treat chickens.

The simultaneous administration of multiple antibiotics has emerged as another strategy to fight antibiotic resistance. It may sound like this would lead to the use of even more antibiotics, but a combination of drugs is likely to pack such a potent punch that resistant bacteria can't develop. Early in the development of effective antibiotic treatment for tuberculosis, it became clear that multiple antibiotics were required to quell the infection because, in a large bacterial population, it was likely that at least one bacterium would develop resistance to a single antibiotic but extremely unlikely that one bacterium would simultaneously develop resistance to two or more antibiotics. This multiple-antibiotic strategy has been used to treat bacterial infections other than tuberculosis. For example, a common antibiotic prescription for urinary tract infections is sulfamethosoxazole and trimethoprim. This combination is substantially more effective than either antibiotic alone, and co-administration of the drugs reduces the development of resistance. Similarly combining an antibiotic-like molecule that inhibits ß-lactamases and a ß-lactam antibiotic has proven effective in blunting some forms of drug resistance. For example, Augmentin® is a combination of the antibiotic amoxicillin with the ß-lactamase inhibitor, clavulanic acid.

This approach hasn't been widely used due to the costs associated with multiple antibiotics and concern for increasing the risk of side effects as more drugs are used. This approach, however, may be very effective against rapid development of antibiotic resistance in some infections. For example a significant number of soldiers severely wounded in combat in Iraq between 2003 and 2005 have developed bone infections caused by *Acinetobacter* species. These microbes are increasingly highly antibiotic resistant, but some of these infections have been successfully treated with simultaneous use of two different antibiotics.

Other efforts are focused on intelligent antibiotic design. This term has two meanings. In one sense it means reversing the normal process of antibiotic discovery. In this reverse process, a scientist starts with structures or enzymes that are unique to bacteria, and designs new molecules that attack them. This approach has been greatly aided by the many completely sequenced genomes of bacterial pathogens. Computer analysis of these DNA sequences allows for the identification of proteins or structures unique to these pathogens. One advantage of this approach is that the proteins or structures can be isolated, and potential inhibitors of these molecules identified in a test tube. This opens up a new window on drug discovery, giving hope that more new, effective antibiotics will be discovered.

The other meaning of intelligent drug design is the use of principles of evolution by natural selection to focus on developing drugs that can more readily keep resistance in check. For example, because multiple mutations for resistance are less probable than single mutations, a drug developed to target multiple bacterial enzymes simultaneously would be more potent than one that targets a single enzyme. Additionally, the development of synthetic antibiotics, which have never been encountered in the environment by microbes, may also lengthen the time for resistance to develop, particularly if resistance is commonly caused by the acquisition of a resistance gene already present in nature.

Scientists can also fight antibiotic resistance by gaining more knowledge about the detailed mechanisms by which resistance develops. A recent report, for example, indicated that the antibiotic ciprofloxacin induces a biochemical pathway in bacteria that increases the mutation rate. This means that some bacteria exposed to ciprofloxacin will more readily develop mutations in the genes targeted by this antibiotic. When the genes in this biochemical pathway are inactivated, mutations leading to ciprofloxacin resistance don't develop nearly as readily. This suggests that targeting the protein products of these genes may augment antibiotic therapy. For example, ciprofloxacin and an inhibitor of this mutator pathway could be administered simultaneously.

Even for the most conscientious health care workers, the decision about which antibiotic to prescribe is often an educated guess. From the time a swab, or sample of bacteria, is taken from the patient, it can take two or more days before the antibiotic resistance profile for the organism is known. Reducing that time to an hour would allow physicians to prescribe only the most appropriate antibiotic for a particular infection, helping keep resistance in check.

Current methods for detecting antibiotic resistance test whether an organism can grow in the presence of the antibiotic. The speed of this procedure depends on the intrinsic growth rate of the microbe, so it is difficult to reduce the current time requirement significantly. Most methods for speeding up the detection of resistant bacteria rely on some type of DNA analysis. A number of DNA-based strategies for speeding up antibiotic resistance testing are currently under development. These methods include multiplex PCR and microarray analysis.

Multiplex PCR uses a chemical reaction to test for the presence of a number of different antibiotic resistance genes. If these genes are found, then the antibiotic they resist will not be prescribed. In a more recent version of this method, the chemical reactions assign a uniquely colored chemical tag to each different resistance gene. A detector in the machine that runs the reaction identifies different resistance genes by color. This technology can complete the reaction in less than an hour, but it is still in the experimental phase. It tends to be costly, requires technicians with highly specialized training, and can be prone to false-positive reactions if samples are not handled carefully. In addition, this system cannot readily detect all forms of resistance, for example, resistance due to single DNA changes.

Another method being developed for rapid antibiotic testing is **microarray analysis**. In microarray analysis, a large number of different DNA molecules are spotted on a glass slide, or synthesized on a silicon chip. These different DNA molecules would represent different DNAs associated with antibiotic resistance. DNA from the pathogen is then isolated, labeled, and incubated with the chip; where the pathogen DNA binds to the DNA spots represents resistance to a particular antibiotic. Antibiotics for which no resistance determinant was found would then be prescribed. This method has the potential to identify more types of antibiotic resistance, compared to multiplex PCR. However, one limitation is getting a sufficient amount of purified pathogen DNA for the procedure. This normally requires growing a pure culture, which slows the process to the same speed as the traditional methods of antibiotic resistance testing.

Development of vaccines for important bacterial pathogens offers another important strategy for keeping antibiotic resistance in check. This would include pathogens such as *Streptococcus pneumoniae, Mycobacterium tuberculosis, Staphylococcus aureus, Neisseria gonorrhoeae, Neisseria meningitidis, Salmonella enterica,* and others. For some of these pathogens, great progress has been made. A vaccine was approved in the year 2000 for preventing *S. pneumoniae* infections in children. Within two years after the introduction of the vaccine, the number of infections caused by this organism dropped 40 percent, including a 15 percent reduction in the number of infections caused by antibiotic-resistant strains of the bacteria.

Much work has gone into developing vaccines for the other pathogens. The genomes of all these organisms have been sequenced, providing many leads for vaccine targets. In the case of vaccine development for *N. menigitidis* and *N. gonorrhoeae,* genomic research is again playing a major role in work toward making an effective vaccine. Typically, bacterial surface proteins are useful components of vaccines, since they are directly exposed to the agents of the immune system. However, in these organisms, the surface proteins that had been identified were quite variable from one strain to another. Consequently, a vaccine containing these variable proteins would not likely protect someone who was vaccinated from most forms of these dangerous pathogens. When the genome sequence of *N. menigitidis* became available, researchers could now identify all the likely surface proteins of this pathogen. Through their analysis, scientists discovered four surface proteins that weren't variable and were also very similar in *N. menigitidis* and *N. gonorrhoeae.* This may allow researchers to develop a vaccine that could simultaneously protect against both of these pathogens. The application of the research mentioned above may further aid in the development of vaccines for *Neisseria* pathogens. Hopefully, this will reduce illness and the number of antibiotic prescriptions required for treating this organism. (In addition, an improved *N. meningitidis* vaccine, developed using traditional methods, has recently been approved for use in the United States.)

Another vaccine-related strategy in development is vaccination specifically directed against antibiotic-resistant bacteria. In this strategy, the vaccine might contain a protein that

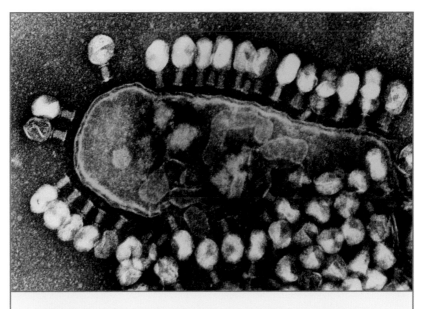

Figure 7.1 Color-enhanced transmission electron microscope image of T4 bacteriophages attacking host (*Escherichia coli*).

pumps the antibiotic out of the cell. Following vaccination, the body would develop an immune response against bacteria containing that resistance protein. If the strategy worked, antibiotic-resistant bacteria would be killed by the immune system, thereby eliminating the selective advantage these organisms normally have over antibiotic-sensitive bacteria.

One final strategy involves new approaches to treating bacterial infections. **Bacteriophages** (bacterial viruses) have been occasionally used, particularly in Eastern Europe, to treat some bacterial infections. Operating on the principle that "the enemy of my enemy is my friend," these bacterial enemies operate by penetrating the bacterial cell, converting the bacterium into a virus factory, then bursting out of the bacterium to go on to infect new bacterial cells (Figure 7.1). Bacterial viruses are very specific, attacking only certain strains or species of bacteria. Therefore, they can be used without harming beneficial bacteria. Antibacterial virus therapy is attractive in principle, but it runs into some practical difficulties. Bacteria develop mutations that make them resistant to virus infection at a frequency similar to that of antibiotic resistance. When viruses are injected into the body, the immune system recognizes them as foreign and targets them for destruction. This immune response would normally only happen after the first exposure to the virus, meaning that therapy with a specific virus could probably only be used once. Subsequently, the immune system would probably destroy the virus before it could attack the bacteria. An exception might be some sites on the body, like the surface of the skin, where the immune system is relatively inactive.

8

The Future of Antibiotic Resistance

But I would like to sound one note of warning. Penicillin is to all intents and purposes non-poisonous so there is no need to worry about giving an overdose and poisoning the patient. There may be a danger, though, in underdosage. It is not difficult to make microbes resistant to penicillin in the laboratory by exposing them to concentrations not sufficient to kill them, and the same thing has occasionally happened in the body. The time may come when penicillin can be bought by anyone in the shops. Then there is the danger that the ignorant man may easily underdose himself and by exposing his microbes to non-lethal quantities of the drug make them resistant. Here is a hypothetical illustration. Mr. X. has a sore throat. He buys some penicillin and gives himself not enough to kill the streptococci but enough to educate them to resist penicillin. He then infects his wife. Mrs. X gets pneumonia and is treated with penicillin. As the streptococci are now resistant to penicillin, the treatment fails. Mrs. X dies. Who is primarily responsible for Mrs. X's death? Why Mr. X, whose negligent use of penicillin changed the nature of the microbe. Moral: If you use penicillin, use enough. [28]

Sir Alexander Fleming, 1945

**Predicting the future is always uncertain, although Fleming was quite insightful in his concerns for the future of penicillin. Many researchers and scientists are looking ahead to some of the issues that are likely to determine whether antibiotic resistance will spin out of control, and some see two possible, alternative scenarios regarding the long-term usefulness of antibiotics. A guiding principle in these scenarios, as described by Stephan Harbarth and Matthew Samore, is that antibiotics are a "nonrenewable resource."

SELECTION PRESSURE ON BACTERIA

The natural selection in favor of antibiotic resistance is a powerful driver of the evolution of resistant microbes. This can't be changed, but the type of selective pressure applied can determine to what extent antibiotic resistance will develop. For example, increased use of multiple drug treatments, the development of antibiotics that target only virulence factors required to cause a disease, and the development of vaccines that reduce the incidence of infection would all be expected to inhibit the development of drug resistance in pathogens. In addition, simple measures focusing on handwashing and other infection-control practices could greatly inhibit the dissemination of resistant microbes. Not practicing these measures widely would, conversely, be expected to enhance microbial resistance to antibiotics and the dissemination of those resistant strains.

CHANGES IN ANTIBIOTIC USAGE

The use of antibiotics by people who do not have a bacterial infection likely enhances the development of antibiotic resistance and may only harm the patient. Close examination of antibiotic-prescribing practices is an important component of dampening the increased development of antibiotic resistance. The vast use of antibiotics in agriculture should also be carefully examined to ensure that these practices ultimately result in the greatest benefits for society. For example, the use of antibiotics of the same chemical class in animals as those used for human treatments requires scrutiny, particularly in cases where antibiotic-resistant bacterial infections can be transmitted to humans from foods. Consideration needs to be taken, though, of the effect these changes could have on antibiotic production and development. For example, if antibiotic prescriptions decline in volume, pharmaceutical companies could see the market for new drugs as being unworthy of future investment.

HUMAN POPULATION ATTRIBUTES

An aging population, with a larger number of immunocompromised individuals, will likely lead to higher rates of antibiotic use. Similarly, the increased use of highly invasive medical procedures will expose more people to the risk of infection. Conversely, improved care for chronic diseases, like diabetes, may reduce some of the risk of infection for individuals with these diseases, and consequently the volume of antibiotic prescription.

Widespread travel and migration have resulted in widespread dissemination of drug-resistant bacteria. Armed conflicts and terrorist actions have led to injuries, which in turn have led to infections with antibiotic-resistant bacteria. In some cases, transport of individuals from one region to another for treatment has led to the importation of drug-resistant bacteria and disease outbreaks in new countries.

With global travel, local concern about antibiotic-prescribing practices has expanded to concern about prescribing practices and the availability of antibiotics over the counter in many countries in the world. This could eventually lead to restrictions on travel to or from certain countries, somewhat like bans on animal export from countries where an endemic disease, like foot-and-mouth disease, exists.

CHANGES IN HEALTH CARE

The number of people with access to affordable and effective health care is likely to have an effect on antibiotic resistance, but exactly what that effect will be is difficult to predict. For example, better preventative care may reduce susceptibility to infection, and thereby alleviate the need for antibiotics. Conversely,

if better access to care means an increase in antibiotic prescription rates, it is likely that this would lead to more selection
pressure and higher rates of antibiotic resistance. Legislation
involving restriction of antibiotic usage in a health care or agricultural setting is another unpredictable but potentially important factor in future trends.

PESSIMISTIC VIEW

A pessimistic view regarding antibiotics and antibiotic resistance is that what is now a serious problem will become cata-
strophic. A slowing rate of new antibiotic development,
coupled with the rapid development of antibiotic resistance
may lead to a "post-antibiotic era." For example, *Streptococcus pyogenes* may develop resistance to penicillin and erythromycin; *Staphylococcus aureus* may develop widespread
resistance to the newest antibiotics, linezolid and synercid,
and frequently acquire vancomycin resistance from enterococci; *Salmonella enterica* DT104 or a similar strain may
develop widespread resistance to ciprofloxacin and newer
cephalosporins. Multi–drug-resistant tuberculosis could
spread from regions that currently have a high incidence of
disease, and the spectrum of resistance could widen. That
would make some of these infections difficult, perhaps even
impossible, to treat. The death rates for these illnesses could
approach the death rates prior to the discovery and development of antibiotics. New medical treatments and invasive
procedures may expand the potential for infection, and may
allow some microbes, previously considered to be nonpathogenic, to become responsible for serious disease. This scenario
could include widespread natural and human-caused outbreaks of infectious disease. These disease outbreaks, in turn,
may result in the widespread use of antibiotics by frightened
but healthy people, exacerbating the current problem of
antibiotic resistance.

WHAT EVIDENCE SUPPORTS THIS BLEAK PICTURE?

The rate at which new classes of antibiotics have been developed has slowed substantially. Between 1936 and 1962 (26 years) seven new classes of antibiotics were discovered. In the subsequent 38 years no new classes of antibiotics had been developed; and only one new class has been discovered since.

Increasing levels of antibiotic resistance have been found, with a few exceptions, for most common pathogens. In some cases, like penicillin resistance in *Streptococcus pneumoniae*, previously rare forms of resistance have become common.

Global travel has contributed to the spread of some antibiotic-resistant infections. This has been the case, for example, for tuberculosis in the United States, which is much more common in foreign-born residents now living in the United States.

Currently, tissue transplants, chemotherapy, and other medical interventions have created a large pool of immuno-compromised individuals. Continued developments in medical science may increase the size of the pool, likely leading to more infections and more antibiotic use.

Incidents in 2001 where anthrax was sent through the United States mail led to widespread antibiotic prophylaxis. Future such incidents are likely to lead to even more widespread antibiotic usage, and the potential for an accompanying increase in antibiotic resistance.

OPTIMISTIC VIEW

A less distressing view is that antibiotic resistance will continue to be manageable, and future improvements will diminish the seriousness of the problem. In this scenario, new technologies for determining antibiotic resistance and more education of patients and physicians will reduce the number of inappropriate prescriptions, thereby reducing the selection pressure for the development of antibiotic resistance. More scrutiny will be focused on antibiotic usage in agriculture, and antibiotic use will be curtailed in circumstances where human health may be endangered. Developments in basic microbiology, such as genome sequencing and analysis, will enhance efforts to develop new antibiotics. New antibiotic development will continue at a pace that keeps medicine ahead of the microbes. The use of new therapies and approaches will lead to a reduction in antibiotic resistance in important human pathogens.

What evidence supports this more positive view of antibiotic resistance in the future?

For most bacterial infections, effective antibiotics are still available.

Educational efforts and legislative measures have been implemented in a number of countries that have reduced antibiotic usage and, in some cases, reduced the proportion of antibiotic-resistant bacteria.

The European Union recently banned the use of a glycopeptide antibiotic for animal use, and the U.S. Food and Drug Administration recently banned the use of fluoroquinolones in poultry. Both of these decisions were based on human health concerns associated with antibiotic usage.

Although the rate of new antibiotic development has declined, important new antibiotics have come on the market recently, and a large market for new antibiotics is likely to spur the drug companies to further development of new, more effective antibiotics. For example, new antibiotics were coming on the market to treat S. aureus infections at about the same time that the first reports of vancomycin-resistant strains were emerging.

Development of a vaccine for S. pneumoniae has led to a reduction in infections caused by this organism; development of vaccines for other important bacterial pathogens may further reduce the need for antibiotics.

Which of these scenarios comes to pass will depend on many factors. The next chapter focuses on steps that you personally can take to try to move toward the more optimistic scenario.

9

Reducing Antibiotic Resistance

Many of the things you can personally do to reduce your risk of getting antibiotic-resistant bacteria involve taking steps to avoid becoming ill. These include washing your hands frequently to prevent the transmission of infections, washing fruit and vegetables, and avoiding raw eggs and undercooked meat. Make sure your vaccinations are up to date; vaccines protect against infections. Become an informed health consumer. Antibiotics are not effective against viral infections; therefore, if you are aware of the symptoms of common viral infections, it will help you understand why your physician isn't prescribing antibiotics when you have one. Don't insist on getting antibiotics from your doctor. If you are given antibiotics, be sure to take the full course of your medication, paying attention to the timing given on the bottle. If you don't, you risk exposing the microbes to low levels of antibiotics that lead to the development of antibiotic resistance.

Responsible antibiotic use has frequently been portrayed as a social good, so it may seem that limiting your personal use of antibiotics may not help you too much, but it will benefit humans as a group. However, a 2005 report[30] suggested that recent antibiotic use by an individual predisposes that person to be colonized by antibiotic-resistant bacteria. If that person undergoes surgery or develops some other condition where antibiotic resistance can become a problem, they can be at greater risk from infection because of their own antibiotic use. Therefore, judicious use of antibiotics can benefit you personally.

Table 9.1 When Do I Need an Antibiotic?[29]

Illness	Usual Cause		Antibiotic Needed?
	Virus	Bacteria	
Colds (e.g., sore throat, runny nose, postnasal drip, cough, fever, laryngitis, sinus congestion, colored nasal discharge, and headache)	X		No[a]
Cough and Bronchitis	X		No[b]
Ear Pain	X	X	Sometimes[c]
Flu (e.g., similar to those for colds PLUS aches and pain, chills, fever up to 103°F, and sensitivity to light)	X		No[a]
Runny Nose	X		No
Sinus Infection	X	X	Sometimes[d]
Sore Throat	X		No[e]
Strep Throat		X	Yes[f]
Urinary Tract Infection		X	Yes

[a] If you have a respiratory illness of unusual severity or duration, your infection may be caused by bacteria. In these cases, your physician may decide to treat you with an antibiotic.

[b] Contact your health care practitioner if you have a prolonged cough.

[c] There are several types of ear infections. Antibiotics are effective for most, but not all, ear infections.

[d] Even if you have a runny nose, or yellow or green mucus coming from your nose, you may not need an antibiotic. Antibiotics should only be used for severe infections or infections that last more than two weeks, since these may be caused by bacteria.

[e] Most sore throats, particularly those associated with a runny nose and cough, are caused by viruses and cannot be cured by antibiotics.

[f] Strep throat is caused by bacteria and requires treatment with antibiotics. Your physician can do a throat swab to determine whether you have strep throat and need an antibiotic.

Source: Tufts Health Care Institute

Having read this book, you are now more aware of the problems associated with antibiotic resistance. Advise your family, friends, and associates about this problem and about what they can do to help preserve antibiotics for us and for future generations.

abscesses—Pus-filled lesions, frequently a symptom of *Staphylococcus aureus* skin infections.

actinomycetes—A group of bacteria, often multicellular and filamentous, which produce a number of different antibiotics

affinity—A chemical preference for one compound over another. For example, many antibiotics have a much higher affinity for a bacterial enzyme, compared to a similar human enzyme.

agar medium—A complex collection of nutrients for bacterial or fungal growth, solidified with agar, a compound isolated from seaweed.

aminoglycosides—A type of antibiotic consisting of modified sugars. These antibiotics prevent bacterial protein synthesis.

ampicillin—A type of ß-lactam antibiotic.

antibiotics—As used in this book, natural or synthetic chemicals, normally taken internally, that are capable of destroying bacteria without harming the human host.

antiseptics—Chemicals that are used to reduce bacterial populations on the skin.

asymptomatic—Without obvious signs of disease.

bacteriophages—Viruses that infect bacteria; the term literally means "bacteria eater."

bacitracin—A type of antibiotic that inhibits the synthesis of the bacterial cell wall.

ß-lactams—A group of antibiotics, including penicillin, that have a four-atom ring. These drugs prevent bacteria from making an intact cell wall.

ß-lactamases—Enzymes that destroy ß-lactam antibiotics, like penicillin.

carbapenems—A type of ß-lactam antibiotic; like other antibiotics of this class, it inhibits bacterial cell wall synthesis.

cephalosporins—A type of ß-lactam antibiotic; like other antibiotics of this class, it inhibits bacterial cell wall synthesis.

chloramphenicol—An antibiotic, in its own chemical class, that inhibits protein synthesis.

ciprofloxacin—A fluoroquinolone antibiotic that inactivates DNA gyrase and DNA topoisomerase, preventing bacterial DNA synthesis.

conjugation—DNA transfer between bacterial cells involving direct contact between a donor and recipient bacterial cell. In some cases, the transferred DNA can include resistance genes.

disc diffusion—A method for measuring antibiotic susceptibility. In this procedure, small paper discs, impregnated with antibiotics, are placed on top of an agar petri plate that has been coated with bacteria. During overnight incubaction, the bacteria grow and the antibiotics diffuse out of the disc, creating a zone of decreasing antibiotic concentration, at a greater distance from the disc. The next day, the zone without any bacterial growth around a disc is measured. The larger the zone, the more susceptible the microbe is to the antibiotic. Frequently referred to as the Kirby-Bauer method, in honor of the developers of the technique.

disinfectants—Strong antibacterial chemicals that are used for reducing bacterial populations on surfaces.

DNA gyrase—A bacterial enzyme that is essential for DNA replication. This enzyme is inactivated by some antibiotics, such as ciprofloxacin.

DNA replication—A process where DNA is copied in cells.

efflux—A mechanism of antibiotic resistance, where the drug is removed from the cell via membrane-bound protein pumps.

erythromycin—A macrolide antibiotic, which acts by inhibiting protein synthesis.

eukaryotic—A type of cell that contains a nucleus and organelles.

filamentous bacteria—Multicellular microbes that form branching structures as they grow. These organisms appear mold-like in a laboratory culture, and many of these bacteria produce antibiotics.

growth medium—A mixture of nutrients that allows reproduction of bacteria or fungi used in antibiotic production.

integrons—Mobile DNA sequences that have the ability to move to new DNA molecules, like plasmids. Integrons are different from other mobile DNA elements in that they typically contain multiple antibiotic resistance genes.

Kirby-Bauer method— A method for measuring antibiotic susceptibility. See disc diffusion.

macrolides—Antibiotics, such as erythromycin, that target bacterial protein synthesis.

messenger RNA (mRNA)—An RNA molecule made from a gene (a functional section of DNA). The mRNA determines the sequence of a protein.

methylation—A process whereby methyl ($CH3$ groups) are added to another molecule. Methylation can play a role in antibiotic resistance. For example, the addition of a methyl group to particular sites on ribosomes can confer resistance to antibiotics that target the ribosome.

microarray analysis—A method for simultaneously detecting the presence of hundreds or thousands of different DNA molecules. Microarrays can potentially be used to determine if specific antibiotic resistance genes were present in a particular microbe.

monbactams—A simple form of ß-lactam antibiotics. Like other antibiotics of this class, it targets bacterial cell wall synthesis.

Multiplex PCR—A method for detecting the presence (or absence) of several DNAs at a time. In the context of antibiotics, multiplex PCR can be used to detect the presence of several antibiotic resistance genes.

pathogens—Organisms, generally microbes, that cause disease.

PCR (Polymerase Chain Reaction)—A chemical process that makes many copies of a fragment of DNA. It is being developed as a method for rapid identification of the spectrum of antibiotic resistance of a pathogen.

penicillin—The original ß-lactam antibiotic. Like others in this group, it prevents bacterial cell wall synthesis.

peptidoglycan—A molecule that is the chief component of bacterial cell walls.

Polymerase Chain Reaction—See PCR.

plasmid—A small circular DNA molecule that frequently contains antibiotic resistance genes.

plating—Spreading bacteria over the surface of an agar medium. This technique is used for some methods of antibiotic resistance testing.

polymixin—An antibiotic that destroys the integrity of cell membranes.

porins—Proteins in the cell membrane that form holes or pores for the passage of materials into or out of the cell. These are frequently sites of entry for antibiotics.

prokaryotic—A type of cell that lacks a nucleus and cellular organelles.

promoter—A DNA sequence near a gene that is required for transcription of the gene.

Glossary

quinolones—A class of antibiotics that inhibit bacterial DNA synthesis.

repressor—A protein that prevents transcription of a gene or genes. Repressors are sometimes involved in the regulation of antibiotic resistance.

ribosomes—Cellular machinery for making proteins.

RNA (Ribonucleic Acid)—A molecule in the cell used for transmitting and processing information.

RNA synthesis—The process of making RNA, an important cellular messenger.

streptogrammins—A class of antibiotics that inhibit protein synthesis in bacteria.

streptomycin—A type of aminoglycoside antibiotic; it inhibits protein synthesis in bacteria.

substrate—A chemical that is a starting point for a reaction mediated by an enzyme. In many cases, antibiotics inactivate enzymes by mimicking the normal substrate of an enzyme.

sulfonamides—A type of antibiotic that inhibits the synthesis of an essential chemical, folic acid.

tetracyclines—A class of antibiotics, chemically distinct by the presence of four chemical rings. This class of antibiotics targets protein synthesis.

topoisomerase—An enzyme that naturally functions during DNA replication to untwist DNA. Some antibiotics act by altering the activity of topoisomerases, resulting in damage to the bacterial DNA.

transcription—The conversion of information in DNA to RNA, using a RNA polymerase enzyme.

transfer RNA—RNA molecules that carry amino acids and decode mRNA, allowing the proper amino acid to be inserted into a protein.

transduction—The transfer of genetic material (DNA) between bacterial strains by bacterial viruses. In some cases this DNA can contain antibiotic resistance genes.

transformation—A process where bacteria acquire DNA from their environment. In some cases this DNA may contain antibiotic resistance genes.

transglycoslyation—Part of the process of cell wall synthesis. During this step, new subunits are added to long chains of cell wall material.

transpeptidation—Part of the process of cell wall synthesis. During this step, cross-links are made between long chains of cell wall material.

transposons—Mobile genetic elements that have the capability to move to new DNA molecules. Transposons frequently contain an antibiotic resistance gene and are probably important for the spread of some types of antibiotic resistance.

Endnotes

1   Based on data from Armstrong, Gregory, Laura Conn, and Robert W. Pinner. "Trends in infectious disease mortality in the United States during the 20th century." *Journal of the American Medical Association* 281, no. 1 (1999): 61–66.

2   Based on the account in Heatley, Norman. "Penicillin and Luck." In Moberg, C. and Z. Cohn, eds. *Launching the Antibiotic Era: Personal Accounts of the Discovery and Use of the First Antibiotics* (New York, NY: The Rockefeller University Press, 1990) 31–41.

3   Based, in part, on information from ScienceWatch. "Making penicillin possible. Norman Heatley remembers." *ScienceWatch Interviews.* Available online. URL: http://www.sciencewatch.com/interviews/norman_heatly.htm. Posted in 1995.

4   Curtis, John. "Fulton, penicillin and chance." Yale Medicine Capsule. Available online. URL: http://www.med.yale.edu/external/pubs/ym_fw9900/capsule.html. Posted Fall 1999/ Winter 2000.
    Sappington, Thomas. "The early days of antibiotics." Yale Medicine Letters Available online. URL: http://www.med.yale.edu/external/pubs/ym_su00/letters.htm. Posted Summer 2000.

5   Walsh, Christopher. *Antibiotics: Actions, Origins, Resistance.* Washington, D.C.: ASM Press, 2003.

6   Modified from Palumbi, Stephen. "Humans as the world's greatest evolutionary force." *Science* 293 (2001): 1786–1790.

7   Based on Table 35.1 Prescott, Harley, Klein, *Microbiology, 6th Ed.* New York, NY: McGraw Hill, 2005.

8   Salyers, Abigail, and Dixie Whitt. *Revenge of the Microbes. How Antibiotic Resistance Is Undermining the Antibiotic Miracle.* Washington, D.C.: ASM Press, 2005.

9   Fey, Paul, et al. "Ceftriaxone-resistant *Salmonella* infection acquired by a child from cattle." *The New England Journal of Medicine* 342, no. 17 (2000): 1242–1249.

10 Anonymous. "Hogging it!: Estimates of antimicrobial abuse in livestock." Union of Concerned Scientists. Available online. URL: http://www.ucsusa.org/food_and_environment/antibiotics_and_food/hogging-it-estimates-of-antimicrobial-abuse-in-livestock.html. Posted 2001.

11 These data are taken from several articles in *Emerging Infectious Diseases* 11, no. 6 (2005).

12 Kolpin, Dana, Edward Furlong, Michael Meyer, E. Michael Thurman, Steven Zaugg, Larry Barber, and Herbert Buxton. "Pharmaceuticals, hormones, and other organic wastewater contaminants in U.S. streams, 1999–2000: A national reconnaissance." *Evironmental Science and Technology* 36, no. 6 (2002): 1211.

13 Gilliver, Moira, Malcom Bennett, Michael Begon, Sarah Hazel, and C. Anthony Hart. "Antibiotic resistance found in wild rodents." *Nature* 401, no. 6750 (1999): 233.

14 Osterblad, Monica, Kai Norrdahl, Erkki Korpimaki, and Pentti Huovinen. "Antibiotic resistance: How wild are wild animals?" *Nature* 409, no. 6816 (2001): 37–38.

15 Perreten, Vincent, Franziska Schwarz, Luana Cresta, Marianne Boeglin, Gottfried Dasen, and Michael Teuber. "Antibiotic resistance spread in food." *Nature* 389, no. 6653 (1997): 801–802.

16 Anonymous. Quoted from Chapter 3, World Health Organization Report on Infectious Diseases 2000. Available online. URL: http://www.who.int/infectious-disease-report/2000/. Accessed on April 5, 2005.

17 Weigel, Linda, Don Clewell, Steven Gill, Nancye Clark, Linda McDougal, Susan Flannagan, James Kolonay, Jyoti Shetty, George Killgore, and Fred Tenover. "Genetic analysis of a high-level vancomycin-resistant isolate of *Staphylococcus aureus.*" *Science* 302, no. 5650 (2003): p 1569.

18 National Institutes of Health. "The problem of antibiotic resistance." Available online. URL: http://www.niaid.nih.gov/factsheets/antimicro.htm.

19 Koch, Robert. "The etiology of tuberculosis." In *Milestones in Microbiology, 1546–1940*, trans. Thomas Brock (Washington, DC: ASM Press, 1998), 109.

20 O'Brien, Rick, and George Comstock. "The first TB drug clinical trials." Available online. URL: http://www.cdc.gov/nchstp/tb/notes/TBN_1_00/ TBN2000obrien.htm. Accessed on March 28, 2006.

21 Klugman, Keith. "Pneumococcal resistance to antibiotics." *Clinical Microbiology Reviews* 3, no. 2 (1990): 171–196.

22 Reinert, Ralf, Susanne Reinert, Mark van der Linden, Murat Cil, Adnan Al-Lahham, P. Appelbaum. "Antimicrobial susceptibility of *Streptococcus pneumoniae* in eight European countries from 2001 to 2003." *Antimicrobial Agents and Chemotherapy* 49, no. 7 (2005): 2903–2913.

23 Pottumarthy, S., T.R. Fritsche, H.S. Sader, M.G. Stilwell, R.N. Jones. "Susceptibility patterns of *Streptococcus pneumoniae* isolates in North America (2002–2003): contemporary in vitro activities of amoxicillin/clavulanate and 15 other antimicrobial agents." *International Journal of Antimicrobial Agents* 25, no. 4 (2005): 282–289.

24 Doern, Gary, Kristopher Heilmann, Holly K. Huynh, Paul R. Rhomberg, Stacy L. Coffman, and Angela B. Brueggemann. "Antimicrobial resistance among clinical isolates of *Streptococcus pneumoniae* in the United States during 1999–2000, including a comparison of resistance rates since 1994–1995." *Antimicrobial Agents and Chemotherapy* 45, no. 6 (2001): 1721–1729.

25 Fey, Paul, Thomas Safranek, Mark Rupp, Eileen Dunne, Effrain Ribot, Peter Iwen, Patricia Bradford, Frederick Angulo, and Steven Hinrichs. "Ceftriaxone-resistant *Salmonella* infection acquired by a child from cattle." *The New England Journal of Medicine* 342, no. 17 (2000): 1242–1249.

26 Helms, Morten, Steen Elthelberg, Kare Molbak, and the DT104 Study Group. "International *Salmonella* Typhimurium DT104 infections, 1992–2001." *Emerging Infectious Diseases* 11, no. 6 (2005): 864.

27 Pillai, Parvathy, James Tan, Joseph DiPersio, Joseph Myers. "*Streptococcus sanguinis* Endocarditis in a patient who received clindamycin for dental prophylaxis." *Infectious Diseases in Clinical Practice* 13, no. 2 (2005): 73–77.

28 Fleming, Sir Alexander. Nobel Prize Lecture, December 11, 1945. "Penicillin." Nobelprize.org. Available online. URL: http://nobelprize.org/medicine/laureates/ 1945/fleming-lecture.pdf. Accessed on April 5, 2006.

29 Alliance for Prudent Use of Antibiotics. "Patient-consumer information on prudent use of antibiotics." Tufts University School of Medicine. Available online. URL: http://www.tufts.edu/med/apua/thci/tmciPatientFacts.pdf. Accessed on April 5, 2006.

30 Hay, Alastair, Michael Thomas, Alan Montgomery, Mark Wetherell, Andrew Lovering, Cliodna McNulty, Deirdre Lewis, Becky Carron, Emma Henderson, and Alasdair MacGowan. "The relationship between primary care antibiotic prescribing and bacterial resistance in adults in the community: a controlled observational study using individual patient data." *Journal of Antimicrobial Chemotherapy* 56, no.1 (2005): 148.

Bibliography

Abraham, Edward, and Ernst Chain. "An enzyme from bacteria able to destroy penicillin." *Nature* 146 (1940): 837. Reprinted in: Joklik, Wolfgang, Lars Ljungdahl, Alison O'Brien, Alexander von Graevenitz, and Charles Yanofsky. *Microbiology: A Centenary Perspective.* Washington, D.C.: ASM Press, 1999.

Abbott, Alison. "Medics braced for fresh superbug." *Nature* 436, no. 7052 (2005): 758.

American College of Physicians. "What you can do to reduce the threat of antibiotic resistance." Emerging Antibiotic Resistance. Available online at http://www.acponline.org/ear/whatyou.htm. Accessed on March 28, 2006.

Alliance for the Prudent Use of Antibiotics. "Patient-consumer information on prudent use of antibiotics." Tufts University School of Medicine. Available online. URL: http://www.tufts.edu/med/apua/thci/tmciPatientFacts.pdf. Posted Winter 2003.

Angulo, Fredrick, Kammy Johnson, Robert Tauxe, and Mitchell Cohen. "Origins and consequences of antimicrobial-resistant nontyphoidal *Salmonella*: implications for the use of fluoroquinolones in food animals." *Microbial Drug Resistance* 6, no. 1 (2000): 77–83.

Anonymous. "Hogging it!: Estimates of antimicrobial abuse in livestock." Union of Concerned Scientists. Available online. URL: http://www.ucsusa.org/food_and_environment/antibiotics_and_food/hogging-it-estimates-of-antimicrobial-abuse-in-livestock.html. Posted 2001.

Archer, Gordon, and Joseph Bosilevac. "Signaling antibiotic resistance in staphylocci." *Science* 291, no. 5510 (2001): 1915–1916.

Bergeron, Michel, and Marc Ouellette. "Preventing antibiotic resistance through rapid genotypic identification of bacteria and of their antibiotic resistance genes in the clinical microbiology laboratory." *Journal of Clinical Microbiology* 36, no. 8 (1998): 2169–2172.

Bergogne-Berezin, E., and K. Towner. "*Acinetobacter* spp. as nosocomial pathogens: microbiological, clinical, and epidemiological features." *Clinical Microbiology Reviews* 9, no. 2 (1996): 148–165.

Borer, Abraham, Jacob Gilad, Rozalia Smolyakov, Seada Eskira, Nechama Peled, Nurith Porat, Eytan Hyam, Ronit Trefler, Klaris Riesenberg, and Francisc Schlaeffer. "Cell phones and *Acinetobacter* transmission." *Emerging Infectious Diseases* 11, no. 7 (2005): 1160–1161.

Bush, Karen, Ken Tanaka, Daniel Bonner, and Richard Sykes. "Resistance caused by decreased penetration of ß-lactam antibiotics into *Enterobacter cloacae.*" *Antimicrobial Agents and Chemotherapy* 27, no. 4 (1985): 555–560.

Bren, Linda. "Battle of the bugs: Fighting antibiotic resistance." U.S. Food and Drug Administration. Available online. URL: http://www.fda.gov/fdac/features/2002/402_bugs.html. Posted September 2003.

Carmeli, Yehuda, Nicolas Troillet, Adolf Karchmer, and Matthew Samore. "Health and economic outcomes of antibiotic resistance in *Pseudomonas aeruginosa.*" *Archives of Internal Medicine* 159, no. 10 (1999): 1127–1132.

Centers for Disease Control and Prevention. "Drug-resistant *Streptococcus pneumoniae* Disease." Division of Bacterial and Mycotic Diseases, Centers for Disease Control. Available online. URL: http://www.cdc.gov/ncidod/dbmd/diseaseinfo/drugresisstreppneum_t.htm. Posted October 2005.

Centers for Disease Control and Prevention. "Know when antibiotics work." *Antibiotic/Antimicrobial Resistance.* Available online. URL:http://www.cdc.gov/drugresistance/community/snortsnifflesneezespot/resources/vbchart.pdf. Accessed on March 28, 2006.

Cirz, Ryan, Jodie Chin, David Andes, Valérie de Crécy-Lagard, William Craig, and Floyd Romesberg. "Inhibition of mutation and combating the evolution of antibiotic resistance." *PLoS Biology* 3, no. 6 (2005): 1024–1033.

Cole, Stewart, Kathleen Eisenach, David McMurray, and William Jacobs. *Tuberculosis and the Tubercle Bacillus.* Washington, D.C.: ASM Press, 2004.

Curtis, John. "Fulton, penicillin and chance." Yale Medicine Capsule. Available online. URL: http://www.med.yale.edu/external/pubs/ym_fw9900/capsule.html. Posted Fall 1999/ Winter 2000.

Davis, K., K. Moran, C. K. McAllister, and P. Gray. "Multi-drug resistant *Acinetobacter* extremity infections in soldiers." *Emerging Infectious Diseases* 11, no. 8 (2005): 1218– 1224.

Doern, Gary, Kristopher Heilmann, Holly K. Huynh, Paul R. Rhomberg, Stacy L. Coffman, and Angela B. Brueggemann. "Antimicrobial resistance among clinical isolates of *Streptococcus pneumoniae* in the United States during 1999–2000, including a comparison of resistance rates since 1994–1995." *Antimicrobial Agents and Chemotherapy* 45, no. 6 (2001): 1721–1729.

Dunne, W. Michael, J. Keith Pinckard, and Lora Hooper. "Clinical microbiology in the year 2025." *Journal of Clinical Microbiology* 40, no. 11 (2002): 3889–3893.

Bibliography

Feinman, Susan. "Antibiotics in animal feed—drug resistance revisited." *American Society for Microbiology News* 64, no. 1 (1998): 24–30.

Ferber, Dan. "Superbugs on the hoof?" *Science* 288, no. 5467 (2000): 792–794.

Fey, Paul, Thomas Safranek, Mark Rupp, Eileen Dunne, Effrain Ribot, Peter Iwen, Patricia Bradford, Frederick Angulo, and Steven Hinrichs. "Ceftriaxone-resistant *Salmonella* infection acquired by a child from cattle." *The New England Journal of Medicine* 342, no. 17 (2000): 1242–1249.

Fleming, Alexander. "On the antibacterial action of cultures of a *Penicillium*, with special reference to their use in the isolation of *B. influenzae*." *British Journal of Experimental Pathology* 10 (1929): 226–236. Reprinted in: Joklik, Wolfgang, Lars Ljungdahl, Alison O'Brien, Alexander von Graevenitz, and Charles Yanofsky. *Microbiology, A Centenary Perspective.* Washington, D.C.: ASM Press. 1999.

Fleming, Alexander. Nobel Prize Lecture. "Penicillin." NobelPrize.org Available online. URL: http://nobelprize.org/medicine/laureates/1945/fleming-lecture.pdf. Accessed on March 28, 2006.

Gilliver, Moira, Malcom Bennett, Michael Begon, Sarah Hazel, and C. Anthony Hart. "Antibiotic resistance found in wild rodents." *Nature* 401, no. 6750 (1999): 233.

Godfrey, Allan, Lawrence Bryan, and Harvey Rabin. "ß-lactam resistant *Pseudomonas aeruginosa* with modified penicillin-binding proteins emerging during cystic fibrosis treatment." *Antimicrobial Agents and Chemotherapy* 19, no. 5 (1981): 705–711.

Harbarth, Stephan, and Matthew Samore. "Antimicrobial resistance determinants and future control." *Emerging Infectious Diseases* 11, no. 6 (2005): 794–801.

Hansman, D., and M. M. Bullen. "A resistant pneumococcus." *Lancet* 2 (1967): 264–265.

Harrison, Polly, and Joshua Lederberg (Editors). *Antimicrobial Resistance: Issues and Options.* Washington, D.C.: The National Academies Press, 1998.

Hay, Alastair, Michael Thomas, Alan Montgomery, Mark Wetherell, Andrew Lovering, Cliodna McNulty, Deirdre Lewis, Becky Carron, Emma Henderson, and Alasdair MacGowan. "The relationship between primary care antibiotic prescribing and bacterial resistance in adults in the community: a controlled observational study using individual patient data." *Journal of Antimicrobial Chemotherapy* 56, no. 1 (2005): 146–153.

Moberg, C. and Z. Cohn, eds. *Launching the Antibiotic Era: Personal Accounts of the Discovery and Use of the First Antibiotics.* New York: The Rockefeller University Press, 1990.

Hedge, Subray, Matthew Vetting, Steven Roderick, Lesley Mitchenall, Anthony Maxwell, Howard Takiff, and John Blanchard. "A fluoroquinolone resistance protein from *Mycobacterium tuberculosis* that mimics DNA." *Science* 308, no. 5727 (2005): 1480–1483.

Helms, Morten, Steen Ethelberg, Kare Molbak, and the DT104 Study Group. "International *Salmonella* Typhimurium DT104 infections, 1992–2001." *Emerging Infectious Diseases* 11, no. 6 (2005): 859–867.

Huycke, Mark, Daniel Sahm, and Michael Gilmore. "Multiple-drug resistant enterococci: The nature of the problem and an agenda for the future." *Emerging Infectious Diseases* 4, no. 2 (1998): 239–249.

Jorgensen, James, Gary Doern, Louise Maher, Anne Howell, and Judith Redding. "Antimicrobial resistance among respiratory isolates of *Haemophilus influenzae, Moraxella catarrhalis,* and *Streptococcus pneumoniae* in the United States." *Antimicrobial Agents and Chemotherapy* 34, no. 11 (1990): 2075–2080.

Kaye, Keith, John J. Engemann, Essy Mozaffari, and Yehuda Carmeli. "Reference group choice and antibiotic resistance study results." *Emerging Infectious Diseases* 10, no. 6 (2004): 1125–1128.

Klugman, Keith. "Pneumococcal resistance to antibiotics." *Clinical Microbiology Reviews* 3, no. 2 (1990): 171–196.

Kolpin, Dana, Edward Furlong, Michael Meyer, E. Michael Thurman, Steven Zaugg, Larry Barber, and Herbert Buxton. "Pharmaceuticals, hormones, and other organic wastewater contaminants in U.S. streams, 1999–2000: A national reconnaissance." *Environmental Science and Technology* 36, no. 6 (2002): 1202–1211.

Krake, Patrick, Fahim Zaman, and Neeraj Tandon. "Native quadruple-valve endocarditis caused by *Enterococcus faecalis.*" *Texas Heart Institute Journal* 31, no. 1 (2004): 90–92.

Kuehnert, Matthew, Holly Hill, Benjamin Kupronis, Jerome Tokars, Steven Solomon, and Daniel Jernigan. "Methicillin-resistant *Staphylococcus aureus* hospitalizations, United States." *Emerging Infectious Diseases* 11, no. 6 (2005): 868–872.

Bibliography

Laxminarayan, Ramanan, and Gardner Brown. "Economics of antibiotic resistance: A theory of optimal use." Resources for the Future. Available online. URL: http://www.rff.org/rff/Documents/RFF-DP-00-36.pdf. Posted in 2000.

Liassine, N., A. Gervaix, R. Hegi, G. Strautman, S. Suter, and R. Auckenthaler. "Antimicrobial susceptibility of bacterial pathogens in the oropharynx of healthy children." *European Journal of Clinical Microbiology and Infectious Diseases* 18, no. 3 (1999): 217–20.

Lintz, D., R. Kapila, E. Pilgrim, F. Tecson, R. Dorn, and D. Louria. "Nosocomial Salmonella epidemic." *Archives of Internal Medicine* 136, no. 9 (1976): 968–973.

Mascaretti, Oreste. *Bacteria Versus Antibacterial Agents: An Integrated Approach.* Washington, D.C.: ASM Press, 2003.

Naraqui, Sirus, Garland Kirkpatrick, and Sherwin Kabins. "Relapsing pneumococcal meningitis: isolation of an organism with decreased susceptibility to penicillin G." *The Journal of Pediatrics* 85, no. 5 (1974): 671–673.

Neuman, K., D. Cox, and K. Bullough. "Transmission of vancomycin-resistant enterococcus among family members: a case study." *Journal of Community Health Nursing* 15, no. 1 (1998): 9–20.

Osterblad, Monica, Kai Norrdahl, Erkki Korpimaki, and Pentti Huovinen. "Antibiotic resistance: how wild are wild animals?" *Nature* 409, no. 6816 (2001): 37–38.

Palumbi, Stephen. "Humans as the world's greatest evolutionary force." *Science* 293, no. 5536 (2001): 1786–1790.

Perreten, Vincent, Franziska Schwarz, Luana Cresta, Marianne Boeglin, Gottfried Dasen, and Michael Teuber. "Antibiotic resistance spread in food." *Nature* 389, no. 6653 (1997): 801–802.

Phillips, Ian, Mark Casewell, Tony Cox, Brad De Groot, Christian Friis, Ron Jones, Charles Nightingale, Rodney Preston, and John Waddell. "Does the use of antibiotics in food animals pose a risk to human health? A critical review of published data." *Journal of Antimicrobial Chemotherapy* 53, no. 1 (2004): 28–52.

Pillai, Parvathy, James Tan, Joseph DiPersio, and Joseph Myers. "*Streptococcus sanguinis* endocarditis in a patient who received clindamycin for dental prophylaxis." *Infectious Diseases in Clinical Practice* 13, no. 2 (2005): 73–77.

Pizza, Mariagrazia, et al. "Identification of vaccine candidates against serogroup *B. Meningococcus* by whole-genome sequencing." *Science* 287, no. 5459 (2000): 1816–1820.

Pottumarthy, S., T.R. Fritsche, H.S. Sader, M.G. Stilwell, and R.N. Jones. "Susceptibility patterns of *Streptococcus pneumoniae* isolates in North America (2002–2003): contemporary in vitro activities of amoxicillin/clavulanate and 15 other antimicrobial agents." *International Journal of Antimicrobial Agents* 25, no. 4 (2005): 282–289.

Prescott, Lansing, John Harley, and Donald Klein. *Microbiology, 6th Ed.* New York: McGraw Hill, 2005.

Projan, Steven, and David Shlaes. "Antibacterial drug discovery: is it all downhill from here?" *Clinical Microbiology and Infections* 10, no. S4 (2004): 18–22.

Reinert, Ralf, Susanne Reinert, Mark van der Linden, Murat Cil, Adnan Al-Lahham, P. Appelbaum. "Antimicrobial susceptibility of *Streptococcus pneumoniae* in eight European countries from 2001 to 2003." *Antimicrobial Agents and Chemotherapy* 49, no. 7 (2005): 2903–2913.

Rosamond, John, and Aileen Allsop. "Harnessing the power of the genome in the search for new antibiotics." *Science* 287, no. 5460 (2000): 1973–1976.

Salyers, Abigail, and Dixie Whitt. *Revenge of the Microbes: How Antibiotic Resistance Is Undermining the Antibiotic Miracle.* Washington, D.C.: ASM Press, 2005.

Salyers, Abigail, Anamika Gupta, and Yanping Wang. "Human intestinal bacteria as reservoirs for antibiotic resistance genes." *Trends in Microbiology* 12, no. 9 (2004): 412–416.

Sappington, Thomas. "The early days of antibiotics." Yale Medicine Letters. Available online. URL:http://www.med.yale.edu/external/pubs/ym_su00/letters.htm. Posted Summer 2000.

ScienceWatch. "Making penicillin possible: Norman Heatley remembers." ScienceWatch Interviews. Available online. URL: http://www.science-watch.com/interviews/norman_heatly.htm. Posted in 1995.

Shea, Katherine. "Antibiotic resistance: what is the impact of agricultural uses of antibiotics on children's health?" *Pediatrics* 112, no. 1 (2003): 253–258.

Shuford, Jennifer, and Robin Patel. "Antimicrobial growth promoter use in livestock—implications for human health." *Reviews in Medical Microbiology* 16, no. 1 (2005): 17–24.

Bibliography

Stelling, John, Karin Travers, Ronald Jones, Phillip Turner, Thomas O'Brien, and Stuart Levy. "Integrating *Escherichia coli* antimicrobial susceptibility data from multiple surveillance programs." *Emerging Infectious Diseases* 11, no. 6 (2005): 873–882.

U.S. Food and Drug Administration. "Withdrawal of approval of the new animal drug application for enrofloxacin in poultry." Office of the Commisioner, FDA. Available online. URL: http://www.fda.gov/oc/antimicrobial/baytril.html#exclusion. Accessed on March 28, 2006.

Visalli, Melissa, Ellen Murphy, Steven Projan, and Patricia Bradford. "AcrAB multidrug efflux pump is associated with reduced levels of susceptibility to Tigecycline (GAR–936) in *Proteus mirabilis*." *Antimicrobial Agents and Chemotherapy* 47, no. 2 (2003): 665–669.

Walsh, Christopher. *Antibiotics: Actions, Origins, Resistance.* Washington, D.C.: ASM Press, 2003.

Weigel, Linda, Don Clewell, Steven Gill, Nancye Clark, Linda McDougal, Susan Flannagan, James Lolonay, Jyoti Shety, George Killgore, and Fred Tenover. "Genetic analysis of a high-level vancomycin-resistant isolate of *Staphylococcus aureus*." *Science* 302, no. 5650 (2003): 1569–1571.

Whitney, Cynthia, Monica Farley, James Hadler, Lee Harrison, Nancy Bennett, Ruth Lynfield, Authur Reingold, Paul Cieslak, Tamara Pilishvili, Delois Jackson, Richard Facklam, James Jorgensen, and Anne Schuchat. "Decline in invasive pneumococcal disease after the introduction of protein-polysaccharide conjugate vaccine." *The New England Journal of Medicine* 348, no. 18 (2003): 1737–1746.

Witte, Wolfgang. "Medical consequences of antibiotic use in agriculture." *Science* 279, no. 5353 (1998): 996–997.

Zhang, H., C. Hackbarth, K. Chansky, and H. Chambers. "A proteolytic transmembrane pathway and resistance to ß-lactams in Staphylococci." *Science* 291, no. 5510 (2001): 1962–1965.

Alliance for the Prudent Use of Antibiotics. "What can be done about antibiotic resistance?" Available online. URL: http://www.tufts.edu/med/apua/Q&A/Q&A_action.html. Accessed on March, 28, 2006.

Levy, Stuart. "Factors impacting on the problem of antibiotic resistance." *Journal of Antimicrobial Chemotherapy* 49 no. 1 (2002): 25–30.

Levy, Stuart. *The Antibiotic Paradox: How the Misuse of Antibiotics Destroys Their Curative Powers.* New York: HarperCollins, 2002.

Mayo Clinic Staff. "Antibiotics: too much of a good thing." Mayo Clinic. Available online. URL: http://www.mayoclinic.com/invoke.cfm?id=FL00075. Posted February 2006.

MedlinePlus: "Antibiotics." National Institutes of Health. Available online. URL: http://www.nlm.nih.gov/medlineplus/antibiotics.html. Accessed on March 28, 2006.

National Institutes of Health. "The problem of antibiotic resistance." National Institute for Allergy and Infectious Diseases. Available online. URL: http://www.niaid.nih.gov/factsheets/antimicro.htm. Posted April 2004.

Moberg, C., and Z. Cohn. *Launching the Antibiotic Era: Personal Accounts of the Discovery and Use of the First Antibiotics.* New York: The Rockefeller University Press, 1990.

Salyers, A. and D. Whitt. *Revenge of the Microbes. How Antibiotic Resistance Is Undermining the Antibiotic Miracle.* Washington, D.C.: ASM Press, 2005.

Shnayerson, M., and M. Plotkin. *The Killers Within: The Deadly Rise of Drug-Resistant Bacteria.* New York: Little, Brown and Company, 2002.

Web Sites

Alliance for the Prudent Use of Antibiotics
http://www.tufts.edu/med/apua/

Animal Health Institute
http://www.ahi.org/

Centers for Disease Control and Prevention (CDC)
http://www.cdc.gov/

National Institutes of Health (NIH)
http://www.nih.gov/

U.S. Food and Drug Administration (FDA)
http://www.fda.gov/

Index

Index

azithromycin, 17
for gonorrhea, 70
mechanism of action,
17
structure of, 17
aztreonam, 16
introduction of, 20
aztreonam resistance,
date of occurrence, 20
AZT resistance, 66

Bacillus anthracis
(anthrax), 36, 97
bacitracin, 18
introduction of, 20
mechanism of action,
18, 25
bacitracin resistance, date
of occurrence, 20
bacteria. *See also specific
types*
acid-fast, 36–37
antibiotic-requiring, 21
Gram-negative, 33,
34–37
Gram-positive, 32,
34–37
bacterial cells *versus*
human cells, 22–23
bacterial ribosome *versus*
human ribosome, 24,
25
bacteriophages
infection treatment
with, 90–91
resistance transfer by,
66–67
β-lactam(s), 15–16
mechanism of action,
15
subgroups of, 15–16
β-lactamase(s), 40
regulation of, 53–55
β-lactamase inhibitors,
40, 86

β-lactam resistance
mechanisms of, 39–40
regulation of, 53–55
biochemical pathways, as
antibiotic target, 30,
31–32
bioterrorism, 36, 97
Borrelia burgdorferi,
antibiotic susceptibili-
ty of, 71

Campylobacter jejuni
resistance, poultry
sources of, 62, 86
carbapenem(s)
classification of, 15–16
mechanism of action, 15
carbenicillin, introduc-
tion of, 20
carbenicillin resistance,
date of occurrence, 20
catheter-related infec-
tions, 79
causes of resistance,
58–67
cefepime, 16
cefoxitin, 16
ceftazidime, 16
mechanism of action, 35
cell(s), human *versus* bacterial, 22–23
cell membranes, as
antibiotic target, 18,
33–34
cell walls
as antibiotic target,
15–16, 18, 22, 23–25,
32–33
production of, 23–25
remodel, as mechanism
of resistance, 42–44,
45, 57
cephalosporin(s)
classification of, 15–16
introduction of, 20

mechanism of action,
15, 35
for *Salmonella enterica*
infections, 83
cephalosporin resistance
date of occurrence, 20
mechanisms of, 56
cephalothin, 16
Chain, Ernst, 11–13
chickens, antibiotic use
in, 62, 86, 98
chloramphenicol, 18
introduction of, 20
mechanism of action,
18, 35
structure of, 18
chloramphenicol resist-
ance
of *Acinetobacter,* 82
animal (food) sources
of, 62
date of occurrence, 20
mechanisms of, 44–46,
46, 56
of *Salmonella enterica,*
81–83
ciprofloxacin, 18
for anthrax, 36
for gonorrhea, 70
introduction of, 20
mechanism of action,
18, 27, 28, 35
ciprofloxacin resistance
date of occurrence, 20
growing problem of, 60
mechanisms of, 42,
44–46, 48, 56, 88
clarithromycin, 17
mechanism of action,
17
structure of, 17
clindamycin
introduction of, 20
mechanism of action,
35

Index

Index

responsible use of antibiotics, 100–102
ribosomal methylation,
41–42
ribosome(s)
as antibiotic target, 23,
25–28
human *versus* bacterial,
24, 25
rifampin, 18
mechanism of action,
18, 31, 35
rifampin resistance
mechanisms of, 42, 56
of *Mycobacterium tuber-
culosis,* 74–76
rifamycin(s), mechanism
of action, 35
rifamycin resistance,
mechanisms of, 56
RNA, ribosome, as antibi-
otic target, 25–26
RNA polymerase, 29
mutations, as mecha-
nism of resistance,
42
RNA synthesis, as antibi-
otic target, 18, 23, 29,
31

safranin, in Gram stain,
35
Salmonella enterica
asymptomatic infec-
tions with, 83
Gram stain of, 36
Salmonella enterica
DT104, 81–83, 96
Salmonella enterica resistance, 58, 81–83, 96
Samore, Matthew, 94
soil microbes, antibiotic
production from, 15
spectrum of activity,
34–37

spectrum of resistance,
48–50
Staphylococcus aureus
Gram stain of, 36
hospital-acquired, 76
penicillin studies with,
10–11, 13
resistance of, 46
Staphylococcus aureus
resistance, 76–78, 96
in children, 76–77
consequences of, 68
economic and health
costs of, 70
to methicillin, 53, 60,
68, 77
multi-drug, 78
to penicillin, 14, 38, 53,
68, 77
regulation of, 53
transfer from
Enterococcus, 79
transfer to other bacte-
ria, 62
to vancomycin, 68,
77–78, 79, 98
strategies to combat
resistance
bacteriophage treat-
ment, 90–91
curtailing inappropriate
use, 85
development of new
antibiotics, 84–85
infection-control meas-
ures, 85
intelligent antibiotic
design, 87–88
limiting agricultural
use, 85–86
multiple-antibiotic use,
86–87
targeting mechanisms
of resistance, 88
vaccine-related, 89–91

Streptococcus pneumoniae
resistance, 80–81
to erythromycin, 80
genes for, development
of, 57
genes for, transfer
of, 65
mechanisms of, 81
to penicillin, 57, 80–81,
97
Streptococcus pneumoniae
vaccine, 89–90, 98
Streptococcus pyogenes,
Gram stain of, 36
Streptococcus pyogenes
resistance, 96
lack or slow develop-
ment of, 71
to macrolides, 71
transfer to other bacte-
ria, 62
streptogramin(s), 18
mechanism of action,
18, 35
streptogramin resistance,
mechanisms of,
41–42, 56
streptomycin
and *E. coli* growth, 21
introduction of, 20
mechanism of action,
17, 25–26, 35
structure of, 17
streptomycin resistance
animal (food) sources
of, 62
date of occurrence, 20
mechanisms of, 40,
41–42, 47, 56
of *Mycobacterium
tuberculosis,* 73–74
of *Salmonella enterica,*
81–83
substrate overproduction,
46, 56

Index

of *Staphylococcus
aureus*, 68, 77–78,
79, 98
teicoplanin as alternative in, 57

Vibrio cholerae, Gram
stain of, 36

Walsh, Christopher, 15
wonder drugs, antibiotics
as, 14

zidovudine resistance, 66

About the Author

Patrick Guilfoile earned his Ph.D. in bacteriology at the University of Wisconsin-Madison. As a graduate student, he studied how antibiotic-producing bacteria become resistant to their own antibiotics. He subsequently did postdoctoral research at the Whitehead Institute for Biomedical Research at the Massachusetts Institute of Technology on the interaction of bacteria and cells of the human immune system. He is now a professor of biology at Bemidji State University in northern Minnesota, where he teaches microbiology and medical microbiology. His most recent research has focused on ticks and tick-borne bacterial diseases, as well as the development of new laboratory exercises. He has authored or co-authored over 20 papers in scientific and biology education journals; his most recent paper described a laboratory exercise using molecular methods for determining antibiotic resistance. He has also written a molecular biology laboratory manual and a book on controlling ticks that transmit Lyme disease.

About the Editor

The late I. Edward Alcamo was a Distinguished Teaching Professor of microbiology at the State University of New York at Farmingdale. Alcamo studied biology at Iona College in New York and earned his M.S. and Ph.D. degrees in microbiology at St. John's University, also in New York. He taught at Farmingdale for more than 30 years. In 2000, Alcamo won the Carski Award for Distinguished Teaching in Microbiology, the highest honor for microbiology teachers in the United States. He was a member of the American Society for Microbiology, the National Association of Biology teachers, and the American Medical Writers Association. Alcamo authored numerous books on the subjects of microbiology, AIDS, and DNA technology, as well as the award-winning textbook *Fundamentals of Microbiology*, now in its sixth edition.